Models for Writing

Teacher's Book 6

Chris Buckton

Anne Sanderson

Series editor: Leonie Bennett

   GINN

Author Team Chris Buckton
Anne Sanderson
Series editor: Leonie Bennett

Bill Ball (Scottish 5–14 Guidelines)
Robert Hunter (Northern Ireland Curriculum)
Beverley Parker and Steve Yates (ICT)

Ginn
Linacre House, Jordan Hill, Oxford, OX2 8DP
a division of Reed Educational and Professional Publishing Ltd
www.ginn.co.uk

Ginn is a registered trademark of Reed Educational and Professional Publishing Ltd

ISBN 0602 296935

04 03 02 01 00
10 9 8 7 6 5 4 3 2 1

Designed and produced by Gecko Ltd, Bicester, Oxon
Cover design by Gecko Ltd, Bicester, Oxon
Printed in the UK by Ashford Colour Press, Hampshire.

Contents

Introduction

Welcome to *Models for Writing*, the first complete programme to deliver Shared, Guided and Extended writing at Key Stage 2 in line with the requirements of the National Literacy Strategy framework. This programme links writing inside the Literacy Hour with extended writing outside the hour in a structured way. *Models for Writing* offers thorough coverage of the NLS writing objectives (*see matching chart on page 10*).

It also covers the requirements of the Scottish Guidelines on English Language 5 – 14 (1991), and the Northern Ireland Curriculum (1996) (*see correlation charts on pages 11 and 12*).

Improving Children's Writing

Models for Writing will help you to improve your pupils' writing across the ability range, bringing as many pupils as possible up to level 4 by the end of year 6.

It helps to improve writing through:

- stimulating model texts that interest and excite pupils
- modelled writing sessions which provide children with a clear structure
- differentiated activities and extended writing
- guided writing sessions that focus on both text and sentence level work.

Differentiation

Differentiation is offered in group and guided activities in the **Pupil's Book**. The activities are flagged with the following symbols:

> **1** Work for **lower attainers**, often supported by a photocopy master.
>
> **2** Work for the whole class. **Lower attainers** are often supported by a photocopy master such as a writing frame.
>
> **3** Work for **higher attainers**.

The lesson plans for each unit (*see pages 38–97*) offer specific guidance on how to work with different attaining groups during Guided writing.

Assessment

Models for Writing helps you to assess children's writing and judge how their skills are developing. You will find guidelines on assessment and annotated samples of children's writing at different levels on pages 21–31.

SAT Preparation

Suggestions for which units to use to practise writing under timed conditions are offered on pages 35–37.

Information and Communication Technology

Models for Writing includes a comprehensive section of ICT activities for each unit (*see pages 102–108*).

In the lesson plans, the **ICT** symbol indicates when an ICT activity could be used for that unit, and cross-references you to the appropriate page in the ICT section.

Structure/Components

Models for Writing has a simple structure which links Shared and Guided writing in the Literacy Hour with extended writing outside of the Hour.

Each Year of *Models for Writing* has:

Pupil's Book containing model texts, guided and supported activities, and extended writing.

Pupil's Book

Teacher's Book offering lesson plans for each unit, curriculum matching charts, assessment guidance, and ICT activities.

Teacher's Book

Overhead Transparencies of model texts and writing frames for whole class teaching.

Colour Overhead Transparancies

Photocopy Masters for differentiation and homework.

Photocopy Masters

How to use *Models for Writing*

When to Use *Models for Writing*

Each unit is designed around two lessons, with an additional extended writing session. You can use **Models for Writing** alongside any other literacy programme by slotting the two lessons into your planning. Alternatively, you could choose to spend more time on a particular unit or theme (*see 'Linked Units' below*) and extend the lessons over a whole week. Each unit focuses on a single writing objective, making it easy for you to see where they fit into your teaching, and making **Models for Writing** an extremely flexible programme.

How each unit works

Models for Writing is made up of 30 units. In each unit you will find:

LESSON ONE: MODEL TEXT

- The first lesson focuses on the study of a short model text from the **Pupil's Book**. (The text provides the model for the next lesson's writing.) Where annotation of the text is required, it is also offered on an OHT.

- Differentiated group activities are offered through the **Pupil's Book** and the **Photocopy Masters**.

LESSON TWO: WRITING

- *Shared Writing* – Shared or modelled writing based on the model text. Writing or planning frames are offered as OHTs where needed.

- *Guided, Group and Independent Writing* – Differentiated group and guided activities. Guidance is given on which group to work with during the guided writing session.

EXTENDED WRITING

- Each unit ends with a suggested extended writing activity, to be completed outside of the lesson.

LINKED UNITS

- Some units are linked by topic or theme, or explore a particular skill at different levels. Opportunites for linking units are highlighted in the Planning Suggestion section of the lesson plan.

How to use *Models for Writing*

A *Models for Writing* Unit

LESSON ONE

LESSON TWO

Model Text

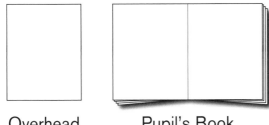

Overhead Transparencies

Pupil's Book

Shared Writing

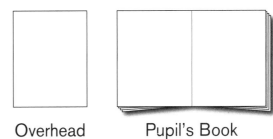

Overhead Transparencies

Pupil's Book

Group Activities

Pupil's Book

Photocopy Masters

Guided/Supported Writing

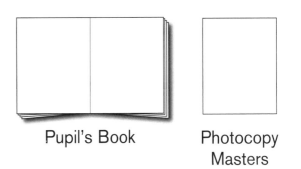

Pupil's Book

Photocopy Masters

Homework

Photocopy Masters

Extended Writing

Pupil's Book

How to use this *Teacher's Book*

main writing objective of unit with reference to NLS framework

unit number

unit heading

text type/ genre

word and sentence level objectives

OHTs and PCMs needed are highlighted

suggestions for exploring the model text

differentiated group activities for the whole class

suggested homework activity

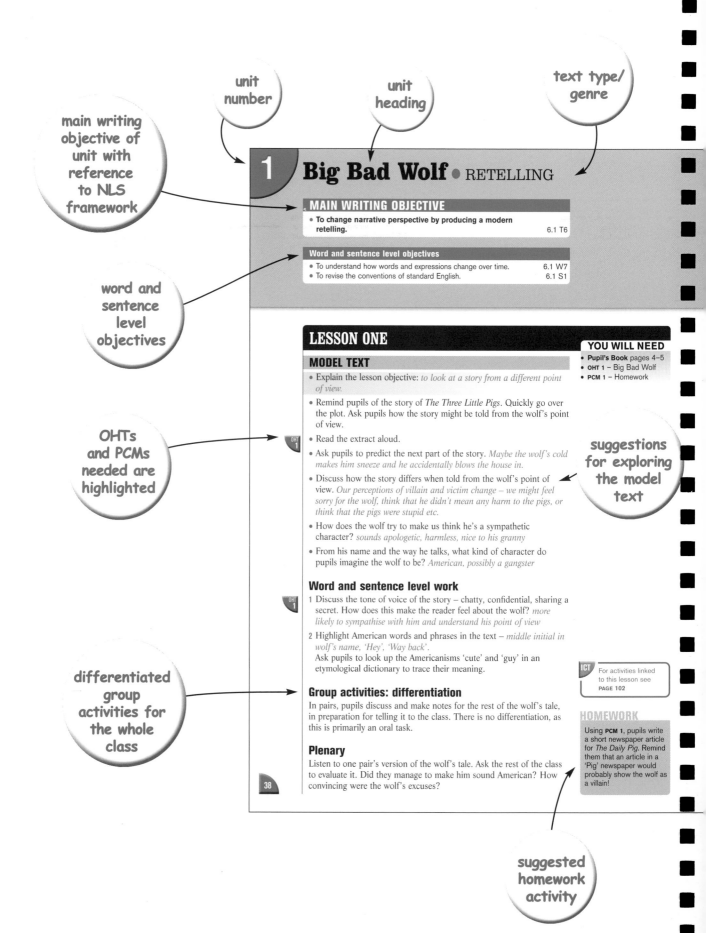

1 **Big Bad Wolf** ● RETELLING

MAIN WRITING OBJECTIVE
- To change narrative perspective by producing a modern retelling.   6.1 T6

Word and sentence level objectives
- To understand how words and expressions change over time.   6.1 W7
- To revise the conventions of standard English.   6.1 S1

LESSON ONE

MODEL TEXT

- Explain the lesson objective: *to look at a story from a different point of view.*
- Remind pupils of the story of *The Three Little Pigs*. Quickly go over the plot. Ask pupils how the story might be told from the wolf's point of view.
- Read the extract aloud.
- Ask pupils to predict the next part of the story. *Maybe the wolf's cold makes him sneeze and he accidentally blows the house in.*
- Discuss how the story differs when told from the wolf's point of view. *Our perceptions of villain and victim change – we might feel sorry for the wolf, think that he didn't mean any harm to the pigs, or think that the pigs were stupid etc.*
- How does the wolf try to make us think he's a sympathetic character? *sounds apologetic, harmless, nice to his granny*
- From his name and the way he talks, what kind of character do pupils imagine the wolf to be? *American, possibly a gangster*

Word and sentence level work
1 Discuss the tone of voice of the story – chatty, confidential, sharing a secret. How does this make the reader feel about the wolf? *more likely to sympathise with him and understand his point of view*
2 Highlight American words and phrases in the text – *middle initial in wolf's name, 'Hey', 'Way back'.*
Ask pupils to look up the Americanisms 'cute' and 'guy' in an etymological dictionary to trace their meaning.

Group activities: differentiation
In pairs, pupils discuss and make notes for the rest of the wolf's tale, in preparation for telling it to the class. There is no differentiation, as this is primarily an oral task.

Plenary
Listen to one pair's version of the wolf's tale. Ask the rest of the class to evaluate it. Did they manage to make him sound American? How convincing were the wolf's excuses?

YOU WILL NEED
- **Pupil's Book** pages 4–5
- **OHT 1** – Big Bad Wolf
- **PCM 1** – Homework

ICT For activities linked to this lesson see **PAGE 102**

HOMEWORK
Using **PCM 1**, pupils write a short newspaper article for *The Daily Pig*. Remind them that an article in a 'Pig' newspaper would probably show the wolf as a villain!

38

links to reading objective from NLS Framework

referenced to Pupil's Book

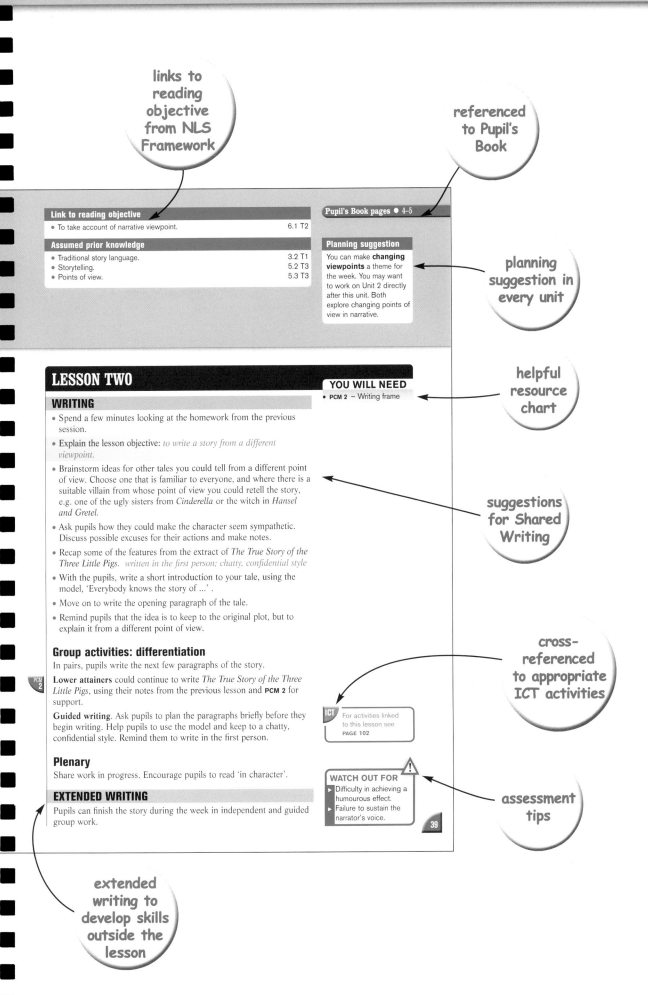

Link to reading objective
- To take account of narrative viewpoint.   6.1 T2

Assumed prior knowledge
- Traditional story language.   3.2 T1
- Storytelling.   5.2 T3
- Points of view.   5.3 T3

Pupil's Book pages ● 4–5

Planning suggestion
You can make **changing viewpoints** a theme for the week. You may want to work on Unit 2 directly after this unit. Both explore changing points of view in narrative.

planning suggestion in every unit

LESSON TWO

helpful resource chart

WRITING

YOU WILL NEED
- PCM 2 – Writing frame

- Spend a few minutes looking at the homework from the previous session.
- Explain the lesson objective: *to write a story from a different viewpoint.*
- Brainstorm ideas for other tales you could tell from a different point of view. Choose one that is familiar to everyone, and where there is a suitable villain from whose point of view you could retell the story, e.g. one of the ugly sisters from *Cinderella* or the witch in *Hansel and Gretel.*
- Ask pupils how they could make the character seem sympathetic. Discuss possible excuses for their actions and make notes.
- Recap some of the features from the extract of *The True Story of the Three Little Pigs. written in the first person; chatty, confidential style*
- With the pupils, write a short introduction to your tale, using the model, 'Everybody knows the story of ...' .
- Move on to write the opening paragraph of the tale.
- Remind pupils that the idea is to keep to the original plot, but to explain it from a different point of view.

suggestions for Shared Writing

Group activities: differentiation
In pairs, pupils write the next few paragraphs of the story.

Lower attainers could continue to write *The True Story of the Three Little Pigs*, using their notes from the previous lesson and **PCM 2** for support.

Guided writing. Ask pupils to plan the paragraphs briefly before they begin writing. Help pupils to use the model and keep to a chatty, confidential style. Remind them to write in the first person.

Plenary
Share work in progress. Encourage pupils to read 'in character'.

EXTENDED WRITING

Pupils can finish the story during the week in independent and guided group work.

cross-referenced to appropriate ICT activities

ICT For activities linked to this lesson see **PAGE 102**

⚠️
WATCH OUT FOR
- ▶ Difficulty in achieving a humourous effect.
- ▶ Failure to sustain the narrator's voice.

assessment tips

39

extended writing to develop skills outside the lesson

NLS Writing Objectives Matching Chart

The chart cross-references the Main Writing Objectives (by Term) against Units 1–30. A ✓ indicates the units in which each objective is addressed.

Units

1	Big Bad Wolf
2	Double Act
3	Eclipse of the Sun
4	Food, Glorious Food
5	I Met at Eve
6	Beowulf
7	In the News
8	Summing Up
9	Harriet Tubman
10	Samuel Pepys
11	Alexander's Story
12	Beach Party
13	What do you read?
14	Zoos
15	Island of Horror
16	All for an Ice Cream
17	Keep off the Grass!
18	Singing my Song
19	Bun Stew
20	The Earth Centre
21	Mountain Adventure
22	Dear Sir/Madam
23	Family Poems
24	Berlie Doherty – Interview
25	How we Breathe
26	Book Blurbs
27	E-mail Etiquette
28	Berlie Doherty – Publishing Poetry
29	In the Stars!
30	Writing to Time

MAIN WRITING OBJECTIVE

	Objective	Units (✓)
Term 1 – Fiction		
T6	To change narrative perspective, through retelling	1, 2
T7	To plan quickly plot, characters and structure of narrative	
T8	To summarise a passage in a specific number of words	3, 8
T9	To prepare a short section of a story as a script	6
T10	To write poems using personification	5
Term 1 – Non-fiction		
T14	To develop skills of biographical and autobiographical writing	4, 9, 10
T15	To develop journalistic style	7, 9, 10
T16	To use the styles and conventions of journalism	7, 9
T17	To write non-chronological reports linked to other subjects	
T18	To use ICT to plan, revise and edit writing to publication standard	1
Term 2 – Fiction		
T10	To use different genres as models to write	11, 16, 19, 21
T11	To write own story using a story within a story	15, 18
T12	To produce a piece of extended writing in one genre	15, 16
T13	To write a parody, using stock characters and plot	12
T14	To write commentaries or summaries, crediting a writer's view	
Term 2 – Non-fiction		
T18	To construct an effective argument	13, 14, 17
T19	To write a balanced report of a controversial issue	14, 17
T20	To understand why standard English varies in different contexts	13, 17, 20
Term 3 – Fiction		
T7	To annotate passages in response to specific questions	
T8	To use a reading journal	
T9	To write summaries of books or part of books	
T10	To write a brief synopsis of a text, e.g for back cover	26
T11	To write a brief, helpful review	
T12	To compare texts	24
T13	To write a sequence of poems linked by theme or form	23, 28, 30
T14	To write an extended story	
Term 3 – Non-fiction		
T20	To secure the use of impersonal writing	25
T21	To use paragraphs to sequence and link text	21, 22, 27
T22	To select appropriate style and form for purpose	27, 29, 30

STRAND	LEVEL D	UNITS	LEVEL E	UNITS
Functional Writing	**Write in a variety of forms to communicate key events, facts or ideas using appropriate organisation and vocabulary. By reading and discussing texts with teachers pupils will identify main forms of functional writing and use them appropriately.** • Write succinctly as appropriate. • Explore appropriate use of notes, lists and diagrams.	3 4 7 8 9 13 15 17	**Write in a variety of forms to communicate key events etc using appropriate organisation and vocabulary.** • Continue to develop skills of selecting and grouping facts from more than one source.	14 20 22 25 26 27 29
Personal Writing	**Write about personal experiences expressing thoughts and feelings for a specific purpose and audience using appropriate organisation and vocabulary.** • Using common situations begin to depict emotions in writing. • Shared writing on board with group to model effective styles. • Look at appropriate style for audience and purpose.	5	**Write about personal experiences in a variety of formats demonstrating some capacity to reflect on experience and with some grasp of appropriate style.** • Pupils have more choice in selecting topics to reflect on aspects which mean more to them. • Introduce form-free verse – haiku, diary, journal etc. • Good models should continue. • Time to discuss writing. • Drama scripts through paired group work. • Poetry – line length, rhythm, form poetry etc.	10 18 19 22 23 24 27 28
Imaginative Writing	**Write imaginative pieces in various genres using appropriate organisation and vocabulary.** • Look at how to turn stories into playscripts etc. • Tell the story in role – newsreader etc. • Look at first and third person narratives in reading material and past and present tense – begin to use.	1 2 6 9 10 16	**Write imaginative pieces in various genres making some use of appropriate literary conventions. Use knowledge of what they have heard and read in own writing.** • Teacher uses questioning to help focus on character development etc. • The notion of openings, turning points and resolutions. • Sections of stories worked on to make up longer stories.	11 12 21 30
Punctuation and Structure	**In the writing tasks listed, punctuate most sentences accurately; achieve some variety in sentence structure, use paragraphs and begin to indicate speech marks in some way where appropriate.** • Use paragraphs to separate aspects of a story. • Use good models to show how sentence structure can create atmosphere, mood and meaning. • Look at a variety of texts for different ways of representing speech – scripts, comics etc.	1 7 13 15 16 17	**In the writing tasks listed, construct, punctuate and link sentences of different lengths and organise them in paragraphs in order to shape meaning.** • Check punctuation etc as part of re-drafting process. Use discussion in pairs and small groups. • Models of correct practice on walls. • Explicit teaching to groups/class as well as in context.	18 28 19 29 20 30 21 22 23 24 26 27
Knowledge About Language	**Show that they know, understand and can use at least the following terms – vowel and consonant, adjective, adverb, pronoun and conjunction, masculine and feminine, singular and plural, tense, paragraph.** • Teacher will introduce the above through contexts and models as well as individual teaching lessons.	2 9 3 10 4 11 5 25 6 8	**Show that they know, understand and can use at least the following terms – main point, topic sentence, evidence, subject, predicate, clause, quotation mark, apostrophe, punctuation. Writing should regularly contain all of the above.** • Pupils will understand all punctuation.	7 14 22 29 30

The strands for Spelling and Handwriting and Presentation would be covered by the teacher differentiating according to each pupil's ability.

Models for Writing and the Northern Ireland Curriculum

UNIT	LEVEL
1	4/5
2	5
3	4/5
4	4/5
5	5
6	5
7	5
8	4/5
9	4/5
10	4/5
11	4/5
12	4/5
13	4/5
14	5
15	5
16	4/5
17	4/5
18	4/5
19	4/5
20	5
21	5
22	5
23	5
24	5
25	4/5
26	4/5
27	4/5
28	4/5
29	4/5
30	4/5

Opportunities are provided for:

WRITING

- Modelled writing
- Shared writing
- Planning, drafting, revising, proof-reading, editing and publishing
- Collaborative work
- Extending vocabulary
- Matching style to form and structure with an awareness of audience and purpose
- Discussing various features of layout
- Presenting and structuring ideas, information and opinions
- Expressing explicit and some implicit meanings and attitudes
- Relating experience and reflecting on ideas, thoughts, feelings and imaginings
- Presenting ideas and information logically and coherently
- Increasing proficiency in the use of syntax and punctuation
- Responding to reading
- Making notes
- Using problem solving to analyse texts
- Experimenting with rhymes, rhythms, verbal play and dialect
- Appreciating the difference between spoken and written language
- Differentiated responses

READING

- Reading aloud
- Recognising some of the effects of a writer's use of language and structure
- Differentiating between fact and opinion
- Using a range of vocabulary when referring to texts
- Using a range of sources to find, select and use ideas and information to investigate a topic
- Modelling writing on forms encountered in reading
- Recognising the main points
- Reading for a variety of purposes

TALKING AND LISTENING

- Engaging in formal and informal discussion
- Collaborating with others; explaining and justifying views and opinions
- Using vocabulary, register of language and detail to achieve particular effects
- Making comments on the appropriateness of their own and others' contributions
- Listening actively and asking questions to develop understanding
- Create and develop a role
- Recognising the different uses of formal and informal language and dialect
- Justifying and sustaining argument, views and opinions
- Preparing and presenting oral presentations

About Shared Writing

In Shared Writing, you, the 'expert writer', model the writing process. Pupils should contribute ideas, calling on their experience of exploring the model text, and you develop them further.

Before Writing

Talk with the pupils about:

- the text type and its features ●
- the purpose and audience ●
- the structure, and how best to order the events or information
- the layout – length, illustration and final presentation
- possible ways of planning – brainstorming, story boards, writing ● frames etc.

What do we know about texts like these?

Who are we writing for?

What is our writing for?

During Shared Writing

- where appropriate, display the annotated model text so the class can refer to it
- explain exactly what you like or do not like about the ideas the pupils offer
- demonstrate how to share ideas and work collaboratively
- 'think aloud' as you write so that pupils understand how to ● consider different options
- demonstrate how writers work at each stage of composition
- show pupils how to apply the conventions of written English – focus on specific aspects of punctuation or spelling
- demonstrate how to revise the writing by re-reading and making changes
- keep the writing short.

I'm making this into a longer sentence by adding extra detail.

After Writing

Show pupils how to:

- talk about their writing; introduce the vocabulary they will need
- edit and redraft their work, perhaps moving larger chunks of text ● as well as adding and deleting words and phrases
- make the link again between reading and writing, considering their work as a reader would – What does it make you feel? What is left ● out or not clear?
- proof-read, checking for sense as well as spelling and punctuation errors
- prepare for final presentation.

Let's add an adjective to describe what he looks like. How should we describe him?

Does this sound right? Is it better if we take out these words?

REMEMBER

Do

- share the lesson objective with the pupils
- emphasise purpose and audience
- refer back to the model text
- direct and control the Shared Writing
- encourage pupils to contribute at their own level
- build on pupils' suggestions
- write with pupils whenever possible
- 'think aloud' as you are writing
- encourage pupils to revise as they write
- teach self-help techniques
- expect pupils to proof-read and edit their work

Don't

- offer unfocused praise
- be afraid to make specific criticisms
- try to correct every aspect of their writing

About Guided Writing

Guided Writing is about providing support for children during the writing process.

For Guided Writing, children should be in small groups according to writing ability. You may teach specific skills, or dip in and out of writing with the pupils, discussing as you go. Providing support while children are working is especially important.

Offer guidance at each stage of composition. On pages 16–19 you will find Prompt Charts to help you guide pupils through each stage of composition.

Before Writing

Help pupils to prepare by:

- reviewing the task ●

  Who are we writing for?

- collecting ideas – maybe by brainstorming or spider webbing
- talking about how to organise the material – choosing key ideas, ● grouping them, putting them in the best order, working out how to link them

  How shall we group all our ideas?

- jotting down words and phrases that might be useful
- checking for gaps in the plan.

During Writing

Join the group when they are already writing. Observe for a while, then:

- find out how it is going and identify any problems
- focus on specific elements of composition, just a few sentences at a ● time

  What could we add to give us more detail?

- remind pupils of the model text and the work done in Shared Writing
- help to develop ideas and build confidence ●
- use appropriate terminology.

  That's a really good connective because…

After Writing

Respond to pupils' work by:

- finding out what the writers were trying to achieve ●

  What are we looking for in this text?

- reviewing the task and recapping the features of the text type
- asking writers to read out sections they are pleased with
- giving precise, positive feedback which lets writers know what effect ● their writing has had on a reader

  I liked the bit when…

- asking writers to identify the parts which need development
- encouraging suggestions for improvement.

Teaching sequence for Guided Writing when planning written work

STEPS	TYPICAL CUES
Review	• What do we know about writing texts like this? • What is the job in hand? • How shall we go about it?
Gather ideas	• What do we want to say? • What ideas do we have?
Marshal the material (select – shape– sequence)	• Which ideas shall we use? • How can we group ideas together? • What order should we put them in? • How can we link the ideas together?
Gather support	• What details can we add? • How can we explain or expand? • What evidence can we give? • What words and expressions come to mind?
Rehearse	• Does it look right? • What are the gaps? • How could we start? • How can it be improved?

Teaching sequence for Guided Writing when pupils are drafting

STEPS	TYPICAL CUES
Review	• What's the task in hand? • What do we know already? • What are the main features of this kind of text? • How did the author in yesterday's Shared Reading tackle this?
Cue in	• How might you start? • Let me start you off . . . • Let's try starting with action this time.
Try it	• Identification • Exploration/generalisation • Addition/deletion/substitution • Praise/building confidence • Assessment • Use of terminology/reflection • Extension/development • Drawing writing into talk
Recapitulate	• What worked? • What helped? • What can we use again?

Teaching sequence for Guided Writing when responding to written work

STEPS	TYPICAL CUES
Recapitulate	• What are we looking for in this piece of writing? • What are the main features of this kind of text?
Read and reward	• What I liked about this was . . . • That makes me wonder . . . • I noticed . . . • Where are the best moments?
Compare and generalise	• Who else tried it that way? • What other ways have been used? • Which of these worked well? • Which tends to work best?
Isolate weakness	• Where are the false notes? • Why does it not quite work? • Which is the hardest part to get right? • What could be improved?
Support improvement	• How could you deal with the problem? • Could we say . . .? • You could try . . . • Start like this . . . • Try writing that part again . . .

Teaching activities: intervening in the writing process

1 Identification/Selection of important features	What I noticed/liked about this was . . . because . . .
2 Addition Deletion Substitution	What can we add? What can we leave out/get rid of? What else can we put in there to make it better?
3 Exploration/Generalisation	The reason why . . . It's useful to know that . . . What tends to work best is . . . because . . . The rule/pattern for this is . . . When else does this happen?
4 Praise/Building confidence	I really like the way you . . . because . . . I really like . . . because . . . That works well because . . .
5 Assessment Assessing strengths, weaknesses Correction	Which parts work best? Why does it not quite work? Which is the hardest part to get right?
6 Use of terminology/Reflection	I really like the term you chose because . . . Which term could you use here?
7 Extension/Development	Could we use, say . . .? You could try . . . You can carry on by . . .
8 Drawing writing into talking	Tell me how you would write . . . So you think that . . . What do you think about . . .? Say a little more about . . .

Independent and Extended Writing

Independent Writing

Independent writing activities flow directly from Shared or Guided Writing. In independent group activities, pupils are still supported by working collaboratively and by using writing frames. (Writing frames can be a powerful support for writers but they can also become a straightjacket. It is very important to show pupils how to adapt them and how to generate their own.) Support also comes from exploring the model text, the preparatory work completed for homework and the Shared Writing session.

Models for Writing also provides **Prompt Charts** which list the main features of each text type or writing process, and these can be displayed for pupils to refer to. (The **Prompt Charts** are located at the back of the **Photocopy Masters** folder.)

Extended Writing

The suggestions for extended writing in *Models for Writing* encourage pupils to carry on with their writing outside the Literacy Hour; to discuss and revise their work; to take their work to presentation standard and, where appropriate, to publish it using ICT. The lesson plans that accompany each unit offer suggestions for how you might integrate the units and the extended writing activities into your weekly planning.

Models for Writing emphasises that writing for different purposes requires different approaches. A shopping list or a quick note will not require redrafting, but a brochure about the school, or a web site, might take several sessions to complete.

Pair and Collaborative Writing: Response Partners

Models for Writing offers pupils ample opportunity to talk about their work and to help each other by giving feedback, as well as times when they can write in near silence. Their feedback will be most effective if they are given guidance and practice in reading each other's work and giving advice on it. Encourage them to act as response partners on a regular basis.

At first their comments may be superficial. They need to learn to:

- find out what the writer is trying to do
- pay attention to content
- identify which features to comment on
- balance positive and negative comments
- be constructive.

On pages 32–34 you will find **Self-Assessment** sheets to support this process. Discuss and model the process in Shared and Guided Writing.

Assessing Children's Writing:
how to improve your pupils' work

Knowing it is good or bad is not good enough!

To reach literacy targets, we need to know *precisely* what pupils need to improve upon. What are the features in pupil X's writing that make him so fluent? What *exactly* are the difficulties that pupil Y is having which may prevent her reaching level 4 by the end of Key Stage 2? If you can diagnose the symptoms you are on the way to finding a cure. Through careful assessment and specific feedback, you and your pupils will find out what they can do already and what they need to do next. On the basis of this you can plan future tasks to take their learning forward. The most helpful assessments focus on a few specific features. Too much information can be overwhelming and de-motivating.

If the learning objective is clear and precise then assessment is easy. Much of the assessment occurs with the pupil during writing, particularly in guided group work. Talking together helps you to find out what the writer is trying to do and what difficulties they are encountering.

Pupils can also get feedback for themselves. Make sure they know the purpose of every writing task and the criteria for assessing it. Show them how to assess their own writing against the criteria and how to work effectively with a response partner.

Prompt Charts

To check whether the piece of writing has the appropriate structure and features for its 'genre' or 'text type', use the Prompt Charts at the back of the **Photocopy Masters** folder.

You can also give these charts to pupils to help them remember the criteria, and structure their writing accordingly.

Self-Assessment

From time to time, ask pupils to assess their own work using **Photocopy Master** A (*see page 32*) and their editing using **Photocopy Master** B (*see page 33*). Children can also use **Photocopy Master** C (*see page 34*) to assist their work with a response partner.

Help them to develop the habit of reflecting on their own writing. If they are involved in setting their own targets they will be much more motivated to achieve them.

Questions to Consider

Purpose and audience

- Is the form of the writing suitable for its purpose?
- Is the writer aware of the reader?
- Does the writing engage the reader's interest?

Structure and organisation

- How effective are the opening and ending?
- How well does the writer organise ideas?
- Does the structure reflect the features of the text type?
- Is sentence construction varied?
- Are sentences and paragraphs joined with a variety of connectives?

Grammar and style

- Is the writing grammatically correct?
- Is punctuation used correctly?
- Are verb tenses consistent?
- Is there unnecessary repetition?
- Does the writing flow?
- Is it coherent?
- Is the vocabulary well chosen?

Presentation

- Is handwriting or word processing clear and suitable for the purpose?
- Is the presentation appropriate?

Spelling

- Is spelling usually accurate?
- Does spelling show knowledge of word derivation, common patterns, and prefixes/suffixes?
- Are guesses plausible?

Writing Sample 1: Level 4/5 Fiction

Fiction: Ghost story
Achievements: Level 4/5
Purpose and audience:
NLS 6.2 T10 To use different genres as models to write.
NLS 6.2 T12 To produce an extended piece of writing.

Summary

The exercise was part of a whole-class SATs practice, planned and written in 75 minutes.
Thomas planned quickly and was confident about the genre and storyline. The writing shows good awareness of the reader.

Structure and Organisation

- A fairly competent ghost story. The opening plunges into the action and the ending is economical and conclusive.

- Events reasonably well-ordered in logical sequence, cutting to key scenes.

- Uses a variety of connectives to link clauses and sentences – when, until – and drives the narrative forward through the use of dialogue.

- Good sense of the dramatic effect of short sentences ('He screamed. He shouted.') and a build up of tension using repetition, dashes etc. (nearer, nearer).

- Creates a sense of speed by using a run of several verbs in a breathless sentence.

Grammar and Style

- Speech carefully punctuated.

- Accurate paragraphing.

- Ambitious vocabulary – 'apparition', 'seep'.

Spelling

- A few spelling errors, but generally these are elements of level 5.

- One or two careless errors, probably due to time pressure.

What next?

- Consider improvements. Cut some of the preliminaries – why so many boys? Extend the panic at being shut in.

- Discuss how to add to the special effects of this genre – adding more details of the ghostly apparition/master bedroom setting.

- Revise rules for punctuating speech.

The Chatsworth Ghost

"Ding-dong" went Mark's doorbell. It was the 24th December, Christmas eve, 1995. "I'll get it" called Mark. "Hello" he said. It was tom and Luke.

"Would you like to come and look round Chatsworth house with us?" asked Luke.

"We're just off to get Jonny," put in Tom.

"Alright," said Mark. "I'll go and get some money". Soon all three were riding down the road on their bikes towards Jonny's house. They picked him up and zoomed off to Chatsworth.

"£5.50 please" said ~~the cash~~ Luke, doing an impression of the cashier.

"Come on you three" shouted Mark. As they walked around the house they realized no-one else was looking round. As they reached the exit they saw that the door was LOCKED SHUT!

Tom looked as his watch. "6 o'clock" he said "They must have closed without realizing we were in here!" Panic struck them. "Come on let's find somewhere to sleep seeing as we're here for the night."

They searched for somewhere suitable, deciding on the "Master Bedroom" as they called it. When they had settled in they started <u>gamboling</u> with a pack of cards Jonny had in his pocket.

"Beat you again!" said Luke as Mark lost all his cards.

"Bet you can't beat meeeeeeeeee!" an eerie voice called.

"I am the ghost of the last Duke of Devonshire."

"Mark, will you shut up" said Luke. But Mark wasn't there. Nor was Tom or Jonny. they were all hiding under the bed from the huge blue mass that was creeping up behind Luke. "It's a bit draughty in here isn't ....iiiiit! said Luke as he turned to face the ghost. He screamed. He shouted. He dived under the bed in sheer terror.

Mark grabbed ~~onto~~ the bed's leg. suddenly the floor gave way beneath them! They fell down, down, down, down, until they landed with a bang on the cellar floor. They could here footsteps, tapping away on the stone floor, getting nearer, nearer, nearer until they were just the other side of the wall – and they stopped. Then a blue, misty fog began to seep through the cracks in the walls and formed into the ghostly apparition they had met in the bedroom It was carrying the cards which Luke has left lying upstairs. The kids didn't hesitate; they ran. They ran fast. And were out in the grounds <u>were</u> they had left ~~there~~ their bikes. They jumped on, rode to the gate, dismounted and heaved their bikes over the wall, climbing ~~over~~ straight over after them. They got on and rode for all they were worth until they got home. they got straight in bed and didn't wake up til ten o'clock the next morning.

They didn't tell anyone what happened – except their parents, who went straight to Chatsworth to complain. The secret lever on the bed was tested, and ~~vis~~ the passage discovered for all.

Writing Sample 2: Level 5 Fiction

Fiction: Poetry
Achievements: Level 5
Purpose and audience:
NLS 6.1 T10 To write own poems experimenting with active verbs
and personification.
NLS 6.2 T12 To produce an extended piece of writing.

Summary

The poem was written after reading poems about the sea and discussing personification.
Paul has a clear idea of the atmosphere he wants to create – personifying the beach. The finished poem shows an awareness of powerful verbs and rhythmic effects. Sharply focused writing helps the reader to visualise the scene.

Structure and Organisation

- Carefully structured, although the ending doesn't quite come off.

- Opening introduces theme – images that follow add to the picture of the beach 'waiting for invasion'. Might have been more effective as the last line.

Grammar and Style

- Good control over construction – use of line breaks and line length to punctuate and create rhythm.

- Well-chosen verbs, mostly used precisely.

- Use of alliteration; assonance -ing endings work well; frozen movement.

Spelling

- This is the final version. Has corrected the few spelling errors.

What next?

- Discuss Paul's intentions – what is 'the invasion'?

- Try reading aloud and make further revisions to the ending – how could Paul personify the sand's reaction to being 'whipped'? Try out some verbs – cowering, wincing. Or try 'waiting for invasion' as a last line: returning to the title, implying that it is people who will destroy the peace.

- Encourage Paul to make observation notes in real landscapes. Give him challenging poetry to read and discuss.

WAITING

All is quiet on the lonely beach
Sparkling shells glitter like bright eyes
Golden sand glistens
Stretching its arms out
Gathered up by the wind
As the waves wash the bay.
Rocks squat silently
Waiting for invasion
Eerie caves open their mouths
Letting out yawns of darkness
Cliffs huddle together
Discussing certain matters.
Water whips the bay
Forcing sand to rise
Forming strange shapes.

Paul

Writing Sample 3: Level 3 Non-fiction

Non-fiction: The skeleton
Achievements: Level 3
Purpose and audience:
NLS 6.1 T17 To write non-chronological reports based on work in other subjects.

Summary

Emily produced this piece of writing after doing some research for a science topic on the body. She has some knowledge of how information books are organised. She presents her work attractively and this engages the reader. Shifts between 'our' and 'your' make it unclear who she is addressing.

Structure and Organisation

- Somewhat scrappy and disconnected because she has tried to cover too much – dots about from whales to humans, jumps to exoskeletons without really explaining the term.

- Hasn't really got a clear enough framework.

- Simple sentences mean there are many aspects of level 2 in this piece.

Grammar and Style

- Doesn't expand ideas beyond simple sentences, although each one is clearly set out as a separate 'mini paragraph'.

- Some understanding of formal, impersonal style – e.g. passive tense.

- Accurate but not sophisticated punctuation.

Spelling

- 'Brake' for break, but otherwise accurate.

- Shows some knowledge of word derivation and spelling patterns.

What next?

- Discuss ways of expanding the sentences into paragraphs. Spend time on planning, brainstorming and then organising using headings and key points.

- Limit coverage and think about using pictures to illustrate key points, rather than just as pure illustration.

- Look at some models.

The Skeleton.

Our skeleton sur...
shape it also f
from injury.

and light so you can move easily.

... in your legs and feet are built for
... support.

Animals that
invertebra...

Animals u
backbo
called vertebra...

protect your heart and lungs.

... a bone. The skull protects the

protects your spinal

Exoskeletons cannot
grow with the
animals so they
have to change
them.

You have 206 bones in your body.

A baby's skeleton has 300 bones that gradually
join.

Bones have to be strong so they dont broke

ORDER NO. ED014052
PUBLISHER GINN & COMPANY
P
QUANTITY   1   DISC: 5.00
TITLE   ORDER BY ISBN
PRICE   23.99
ISBN   0602296935
5649622090

Non-fiction: Mouth to Stomach
Achievements: Level 4/5
Purpose and audience:
NLS 6.3 T20 To secure control of impersonal writing.
An explanation of the digestive system, linked to work in science.

Summary

Lauren has a sound grasp of how to plan explanatory writing. She has enough subject knowledge to be able to concentrate on style and organisation. She speaks directly to the reader.

Structure and Organisation

- Carefully planned and organised – opening introduces the subject; terminology is defined, and there is a logical sequence.

- No paragraphs are used, but the points are ordered in a clear and logical manner.

Grammar and Style

- Appropriate impersonal style – use of passive verbs, 'to be chewed'.

- Consistent use of the present tense.

- Confident in the use of technical terms.

- Very clear.

Spelling

- Only error is omission of 'u' in squeeze.

What next?

- Could explore the use of causal connectives, maybe using a writing frame to emphasise the aspect of explaining *why* as well as how.

- Discuss the use of diagrams and layout – bullet points, numbers, sub-headings etc.

- Paragraphing – may be developed into a longer piece, covering the whole digestive process.

- Check 'qu' spelling rule.

Mouth to Stomach

The digestive process begins when food enters your mouth. The minute you take a bite your mouth begins to produce saliva. The tongue pushes the food towards your teeth to be chewed. Your teeth then grind the food into small pieces. The saliva and the enzymes in your mouth help to break down the food. Then the food travels down the gullet. The gullet is approximately 3cm wide and 25 cm long. The muscles of the gullet contract and sqeeze the food down. The sqeezing of the muscles is called perestalsis. Then the food enters the stomach.

Self-assessment

Title of writing: _____

What was the task? _____

_____

_____

How difficult was it? (Circle the score out of 10)

    1   2   3   4   5   6   7   8   9   10

How happy are you with it? (Circle the score out of 10)

    1   2   3   4   5   6   7   8   9   10

What do you think you have done well?

_____

_____

What didn't work?

_____

_____

What did your response partner say about it?

_____

_____

Do you agree?

_____

What is your new target?

_____

_____

Editing checklist

Remember to check:	checked ✓
Are there enough details to help the reader?	☐
Have you used capital letters and punctuation?	☐
Is speech set out correctly?	☐
Do all verbs and nouns agree?	☐
Are all spellings correct?	☐
Are there any repeated phrases or unneccessary words that you can take out?	☐

Working with a response partner

Read your work aloud.

Is it interesting/enjoyable?

Is anything not clear? List below.

-
-
-

Is anything missing? List below.

-
-
-

Can you suggest:

- alternative words or expressions?

- a better beginning or ending?

Is it too long or too short?

Can anything be cut? If so, what?

Has the writer done what he or she was asked to do?

Models for Writing and Year 6 SATs practice

The six pieces of writing below can be set under timed conditions. It is a good idea to set one piece of timed writing every half term. Give the pupils 15 minutes to plan the task and 45 minutes to complete their writing.

Unit 1 Big Bad Wolf

TASK: Write a modern version of a well-known story, and tell the story from a different viewpoint to the usual narrator.

Assessment Criteria

Purpose and audience
- Is the form of writing suitable for the purpose?

Structure and organisation
- Does it have a strong opening paragraph?
- Does it keep to the original plot?

Grammar and style
- Is it written in a chatty, confidential, humourous style?
- Is it written in first person?
- Does writing sustain narrator's voice?
- Does writing make character seem sympathetic?

Unit 10 Samuel Pepys

TASK: Imagine you lived through a famous historical event and kept a diary at the time. Write diary entries about the episode.

Assessment Criteria

Purpose and audience
- Is the form of writing suitable for the purpose?

Structure and organisation
- Does the writing keep to the historical detail of the event?
- Does it contain personal experience?

Grammar and style
- Is it written in the first person?
- Does it include: active verbs, adjectives and nouns?
- Does writing use precise detail?

Unit 14 Zoos

TASK: Write a report about wearing school uniform, setting out both sides of the argument

Assessment Criteria

Purpose and audience

• Is the form of writing suitable for the purpose?

Structure and organisation

• Does writing begin with introduction to the issue?
• Does it include an argument and counter-argument?
• Does it have a short conclusion?
• Is it structured using paragraphs?

Grammar and style

• Does it use persuasive language?
• Is the writing unbiased?

Unit 20 The Earth Centre

TASK: Write a guide book to your school for parents.

Assessment Criteria

Purpose and audience

• Is the form of writing suitable for the purpose?
• Is it written with the audience in mind?

Structure and organisation

• Is the writing organised into sections?
• Does it make good use of headings?
• Does it include facts and opinions?

Grammar and style

• Does writing include use of imperatives?
• Is it written using persuasive language?

Unit 26 Book Blurbs

TASK: Write a back cover blurb for your favourite fiction book.

Assessment Criteria

Purpose and audience
- Is the form of writing suitable for the purpose?
- Is the writing succinct?

Structure and organisation
- Does it include a brief outline of the plot?
- Does it include quotes from the book?
- Does it use leader dots?
- Does it mention the author?

Grammar and style
- Does the blurb make good use of questions/cliff-hangers?
- Does the blurb make good use of capitals and different handwriting styles?
- Does writing reflect the style and tone of book?

Unit 29 In the Stars!

TASK: Write two horoscopes for inclusion in a daily newspaper.

Assessment Criteria

Purpose and audience
- Is the form of writing suitable for purpose?
- Is it written with the audience in mind?

Structure and organisation
- Does writing adopt the correct layout?
- Does it use correct symbols for zodiac signs?
- Does it address the reader?
- Does it make good use of general themes e.g. love, money etc?

Grammar and style
- Does writing use generalisations effectively?
- Does it adopt an appropriate tone of voice?
- Does it include idioms, dire hints and good news?

1

Big Bad Wolf ● RETELLING

MAIN WRITING OBJECTIVE

- **To change narrative perspective by producing a modern retelling.**
  6.1 T6

Word and sentence level objectives

- To understand how words and expressions change over time.   6.1 W7
- To revise the conventions of standard English.   6.1 S1

LESSON ONE

YOU WILL NEED

- **Pupil's Book** pages 4–5
- **OHT 1** – Big Bad Wolf
- **PCM 1** – Homework

MODEL TEXT

- Explain the lesson objective: *to look at a story from a different point of view.*

- Remind pupils of the story of *The Three Little Pigs*. Quickly go over the plot. Ask pupils how the story might be told from the wolf's point of view.

- Read the extract aloud.

- Ask pupils to predict the next part of the story. *Maybe the wolf's cold makes him sneeze and he accidentally blows the house in.*

- Discuss how the story differs when told from the wolf's point of view. *Our perceptions of villain and victim change – we might feel sorry for the wolf, think that he didn't mean any harm to the pigs, or think that the pigs were stupid etc.*

- How does the wolf try to make us think he's a sympathetic character? *sounds apologetic, harmless, nice to his granny*

- From his name and the way he talks, what kind of character do pupils imagine the wolf to be? *American, possibly a gangster*

Word and sentence level work

1 Discuss the tone of voice of the story – chatty, confidential, sharing a secret. How does this make the reader feel about the wolf? *more likely to sympathise with him and understand his point of view*

2 Highlight American words and phrases in the text – *middle initial in wolf's name, 'Hey', 'Way back'.*
Ask pupils to look up the Americanisms 'cute' and 'guy' in an etymological dictionary to trace their meaning.

Group activities: differentiation

In pairs, pupils discuss and make notes for the rest of the wolf's tale, in preparation for telling it to the class. There is no differentiation, as this is primarily an oral task.

Plenary

Listen to one pair's version of the wolf's tale. Ask the rest of the class to evaluate it. Did they manage to make him sound American? How convincing were the wolf's excuses?

 For activities linked to this lesson see **PAGE 102**

HOMEWORK

Using **PCM 1**, pupils write a short newspaper article for *The Daily Pig*. Remind them that an article in a 'Pig' newspaper would probably show the wolf as a villain!

Link to reading objective	
● To take account of narrative viewpoint.	6.1 T2

Assumed prior knowledge	
● Traditional story language.	3.2 T1
● Storytelling.	5.2 T3
● Points of view.	5.3 T3

Planning suggestion

You can make **changing viewpoints** a theme for the week. You may want to work on Unit 2 directly after this unit. Both explore changing points of view in narrative.

LESSON TWO

WRITING

● Spend a few minutes looking at the homework from the previous session.

● Explain the lesson objective: *to write a story from a different viewpoint.*

● Brainstorm ideas for other tales you could tell from a different point of view. Choose one that is familiar to everyone, and where there is a suitable villain from whose point of view you could retell the story, e.g. one of the ugly sisters from *Cinderella* or the witch in *Hansel and Gretel.*

● Ask pupils how they could make the character seem sympathetic. Discuss possible excuses for their actions and make notes.

● Recap some of the features from the extract of *The True Story of the Three Little Pigs. written in the first person; chatty, confidential style*

● With the pupils, write a short introduction to your tale, using the model, 'Everybody knows the story of ...' .

● Move on to write the opening paragraph of the tale.

● Remind pupils that the idea is to keep to the original plot, but to explain it from a different point of view.

Group activities: differentiation

In pairs, pupils write the next few paragraphs of the story.

Lower attainers could continue to write *The True Story of the Three Little Pigs*, using their notes from the previous lesson and **PCM 2** for support.

Guided writing. Ask pupils to plan the paragraphs briefly before they begin writing. Help pupils to use the model and keep to a chatty, confidential style. Remind them to write in the first person.

Plenary

Share work in progress. Encourage pupils to read 'in character'.

EXTENDED WRITING

Pupils can finish the story during the week in independent and guided group work.

YOU WILL NEED

● **PCM 2** – Writing frame

PCM 2

ICT For activities linked to this lesson see **PAGE 102**

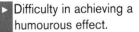

WATCH OUT FOR

▶ Difficulty in achieving a humourous effect.
▶ Failure to sustain the narrator's voice.

2

Double Act • NARRATION

MAIN WRITING OBJECTIVE

- **To write a story with two narrators.** 6.1 T6

Word and sentence level objective

- To use connecting words and phrases. 6.1 S4

LESSON ONE

MODEL TEXT

- Introduce the lesson objective: *to describe a scene from two different viewpoints.*

- Explain that stories differ, depending on who is telling them. You can sometimes tell the same story from different points of view.

- **PB** Read the first extract aloud. This is where the two characters/narrators introduce themselves.

- Ask pupils if they can tell which twin is which by looking at the illustration, and to give reasons for their choice. *Ruby – hands on hips, bold looking; Garnet – meeker*

- Discuss how the author shows which twin is speaking. *italics for Garnet; roman type for Ruby*

- **PB** Read the second extract aloud.

- Discuss the differences in character. *Ruby is the dominant personality, lively and outgoing, always takes the lead, bosses her sister; Garnet is shy, likes to do quiet things like read.*

- Ask pupils how the twins' personalities affect their point of view about the audition. *Ruby is excited, can't wait to take the stage; Garnet is frightened and reluctant.*

Word and sentence level work

OHT 2 1 Look at the first extract in detail. Underline examples of informal, chatty language – *contractions: 'we're', 'I'm'; incomplete sentences: 'Well, until we start talking'; colloquialisms: 'I tend to go on and on'.*

2 Make the language more formal by rewriting the short sentences as a more complex narrative. Model the use of connectives and change slang into more formal language. Use the third person.

Group activities: differentiation

All pupils complete question 1. **Higher attainers** also do question 2.

Guided reading. Work with **lower attainers** to help them think about how character affects point of view.

Plenary

Read and evaluate two pupils' accounts of the audition. Have they conveyed the different personalities?

YOU WILL NEED

- **Pupil's Book** pages 7–8
- **OHT 2** – Extract 1
- **PCM 3** – Homework: Different viewpoints

 ICT For activities linked to this lesson see **PAGE 102**

HOMEWORK

Pupils use **PCM 3** to make notes about an event from two different viewpoints.

Link to reading objective

- To take account of viewpoint in a novel.   6.1 T2

Assumed prior knowledge

- Point of view.   5.3 T3
- First and third person.   5.1 S8
- Other stories by Jacqueline Wilson.

Planning suggestion

Unit 1 is excellent preparation for this unit. You could work on both units in the same week.

LESSON TWO

WRITING

YOU WILL NEED

- **OHT 3** – Planning frame
- **PCM 4** – Planning frame

- Introduce the lesson objective: *to plan a story with two narrators.*

- Explain that you are going to write about a playground dispute from the point of view of two different narrators.

- Recap the work done yesterday and ask one or two pupils to read out their homework notes.

- Discuss an outline plan for your story using pupils' suggestions. As you talk, make brief notes in the appropriate box on **OHT 3**.

- Who are the narrators? What kind of characters are they? What will be their point of view? Remind pupils that a narrator does not have to be part of the action.

- Discuss what might have led to the dispute. It is important to give characters convincing motives for what they do.

- Discuss how the pupils will show the two different narrators: *e.g. separate sections or paragraphs? through their diaries? letters to friends? interview with headteacher?*

Group activities: differentiation

All pupils complete both questions, using their homework notes as the basis for their own story.

Lower attainers can use **PCM 4** to support their planning.

Guided writing. *Either* focus on different ways of conveying different viewpoints *or* work with a group of low attainers and scribe a group story for them.

For activities linked to this lesson see **PAGE 102**

Plenary

Ask pupils to describe their two narrators and why they see things differently. Read aloud some work in progress.

EXTENDED WRITING

Pupils can continue with the first draft of their story. In future lessons, they can work with a writing partner, reading and revising their stories and producing a final version.

WATCH OUT FOR
▶ Difficulty in sustaining different viewpoints, e.g. distinctive language for different characters.

3 Eclipse of the Sun

● NON-CHRONOLOGICAL REPORT

MAIN WRITING OBJECTIVE

- **To write non-chronological reports linked to other subjects.**   6.1 T17

Word and sentence level objectives

- To revise active and passive verbs.   6.1 S2
- To note how changes from active to passive affect word order.   6.1 S3

LESSON ONE

MODEL TEXT

- Explain the lesson objective: *to look at the features of non-chronological reports.*

- Refer to the features on **Prompt Chart 1**, making sure that pupils know what they mean.

- Look at the title of the report. Ask pupils what they already know about a solar eclipse? Make notes under the heading, *What we know.*

- Read aloud the opening paragraph of the report. Ask pupils what the purpose of this paragraph is. *to introduce the subject*

- Now read the second paragraph. Ask pupils:

  – What features of a non-chronological report are included in this paragraph? *a general statement, e.g. what happens when; present tense; impersonal language*

  – Can you think of a suitable heading for paragraph 2? *e.g. general description of an eclipse*

- Look at the diagram. What is the purpose of the diagram? *shows what happens more clearly; makes the written report easier to understand*

Word and sentence level work

1 Point to an example of a passive verb in the extract: *the sun is completely covered.* Change this into active form: *the moon completely covers the sun.*

2 Point to an example of an active verb: *the moon masks out the sun.* Change it into passive form: *the sun is masked by the moon.*

3 Discuss how a change from active to passive changes the order of words and affects the formality of a text.

Group activities: differentiation

In pairs, all pupils complete questions 1–3. **Higher attainers** can move on to question 4.

Guided reading. Read through the report with **lower attainers** and help them to pick out the key facts.

Plenary

Ask pupils what they have learned from reading the report. Note this under the heading *What we learned.*

YOU WILL NEED

- **Pupil's Book** pages 10–11
- **Prompt Chart 1** – Non-chronological reports
- Flipchart headed: *What we know What we learned*
- **OHT 4** – Eclipse of the Sun
- **PCM 5** – Homework

ICT For activities linked to this lesson see **PAGE 102**

HOMEWORK

Pupils prepare to write a report of their own linked to another subject. Give them a title for the report. They should use **PCM 5** to list what they know and what they need to find out before writing the report.

Link to reading objective	
● To understand the features of non-chronological reports.	6.1 T13

Assumed prior knowledge	
● Notemaking.	5.3 T16
● Planning non-chronological reports.	5.2 T22
● Acknowledging sources.	5.2 T23

Planning suggestion

This unit can be used to begin a week researching and writing **non-chronological reports** linked to another subject or class topic.

LESSON TWO

WRITING

- Explain the lesson objective: *to write a non-chronological report.*

- From their homework notes, ask pupils to say what they know about the subject. List the answers on the flipchart, under the heading *What we know*. Discuss any facts which are doubtful and emphasise that they must be checked later.

- Ask pupils what they feel they need to find out more about before they can write. Make these into a list of questions to be answered.

- Ask pupils to suggest paragraph headings for the report. Select the most suitable, and write them on the report planning frame. This will guide pupils' own writing and research.

- Look at the first paragraph heading. Ask pupils to scan the *What we know* points to find facts that fit under that heading. Note these, under *Key Points*.

- Tell pupils that they will work on their report plans in group activities, using the notes from shared writing.

Group activities: differentiation

Pupils use **PCM 6** to plan their report. **Higher attainers** can begin to research answers to the questions listed under *What we need to find out*.

Guided writing. Talk through key points for each paragraph. Ask pupils how these might be turned into sentences.

Plenary

Refer to each paragraph in turn, asking pupils to give key points. Discuss what information is still needed, and suggest they use books and other sources to find this.

EXTENDED WRITING

Pupils finish researching their report, and plan and write the first draft. They can use **Prompt Chart** to help them. They then swap drafts with a partner, and check for impersonal pronouns and the present tense. Pupils then edit and revise their own work before producing a final copy.

YOU WILL NEED

- Flipchart headed:
  What we know
  What we need to find out
- **OHT 5** – Report planning frame
- **PCM 6** – Report planning frame
- **Prompt Chart 1** – Non-chronological report

 For activities linked to this lesson see **PAGE 102**

 **WATCH OUT FOR**
- ▶ Use of personal pronouns.
- ▶ Inappropriate use of past tense.
- ▶ More than one focus in a paragraph.

43

4

Food, Glorious Food

● AUTOBIOGRAPHY

MAIN WRITING OBJECTIVE

● **To develop the skills of autobiographical writing.**	6.1 T14

Word and sentence level objectives

● To understand how new words have been added to language.	6.1 W9
● To adapt texts for particular readers.	6.1 S1
● Complex sentences.	6.1 S5

LESSON ONE

MODEL TEXT

- Introduce the lesson objective: *to look at autobiographical writing.*

- Using the **Prompt Chart** discuss the features of an autobiography.

- Explain that the two extracts describe different places and different times, but are both about food. The first one is from an autobiography by Floella Benjamin, an actress and children's writer.

PB
- Read aloud the extract *Coming to England*.

- The second extract is by Victoria Massey. In it she describes what it was like growing up during the Second World War. Read aloud the extract *One Child's War*.

- Ask pupils for personal reactions to the extracts:

  – Which food do you most like the sound of?

  – Which do you not like the sound of?

- Ask pupils to pick out details that help them to really imagine the scenes and the tastes.

Word and sentence level work

PB
1 Explore some of the less familiar words in the first extract: *brown down, plantains, callaloo, cassavas, gungo peas, soursop juice.* Ask pupils to try to guess what they are. Then look them up in a dictionary or recipe book.

2 Both extracts are written in a chatty style, as if talking aloud. Ask pupils to find some examples, e.g *the use of dashes; contractions – 'didn't', 'it's likely'; slang and exclamation marks – 'Smashing!'*

3 Why are the pieces written in this way? Relate the discussion to purpose and audience.

Group activities: differentiation

All pupils aim to complete both questions, but **lower attainers** may not finish question 2. Differentiation will be by outcome.

Plenary

Ask pupils to read out their descriptions of messing about with food. Take a vote on whether pupils prefer Floella's food or Victoria's and why.

YOU WILL NEED

- **Pupil's Book** pages 13–14
- **Prompt Chart 2** – Biography and Autobiography
- **PCM 7** – Homework: A meal to remember!

ICT For activities linked to this lesson see **PAGE 102**

HOMEWORK

Ask pupils to make notes about a meal they really remember – either because it was fantastic or because they hated it! They can use **PCM 7** to help them.

Link to reading objective

- To distinguish between biography and autobiography.   6.1 T11

Assumed prior knowledge

- Personal writing – recounts   5.1 T24

Planning suggestion

You can make **autobiographies** a theme for the week. This unit could be linked to Unit 9, which explores biography.

LESSON TWO

WRITING

- Remind pupils of the autobiographical writing in the previous lesson.

- Explain the lesson objective: *to write autobiographically on the subject of food.*

- Ask pupils to feedback from their homework notes about a meal they really remember. Add a memory of your own about a meal you really enjoyed.

- Begin to describe the food you had in detail. Focus on its smell, its appearance, its taste and its texture, and how it made you feel. Make it as mouth-watering as possible.

- Ask pupils to contribute words and phrases that describe the food. Jot down any particularly vivid words they use. Comment on why those words work so well.

- Using the writing frame, begin to model your autobiographical account of a favourite meal. Focus on the description of the food, turning the notes made above into more complex sentences. Make sure the account is personal. Use a chatty style.

Group activities: differentiation

Pupils use their homework notes to write about a meal they remember. Remind them to focus on the food.

Lower attainers can use the writing frame on **PCM 8** for support.

Guided writing. Encourage pupils to concentrate on sense, impressions and personal feelings. Look at the style of the writing. Promote the use of complex sentences.

Plenary

Read out one pupil's first draft. How good is the description of the food? Does it make your mouth water? Or your stomach turn? Is it written in a chatty style?

EXTENDED WRITING

Pupils swap work with a partner to see how their writing can be improved. They then revise their first draft.

YOU WILL NEED

- **OHT 6** – Writing frame
- **PCM 8** – Writing frame

For activities linked to this lesson see **PAGE 102**

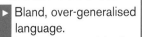
WATCH OUT FOR
- ► Bland, over-generalised language.
- ► Lack of personal feeling in descriptions

5

I Met at Eve • PERSONIFICATION

MAIN WRITING OBJECTIVE

- **To write own poems, experimenting with active verbs and personification.** 6.1 T10

Word and sentence level objectives

- To understand how words have changed over time. 6.1 W7
- To use an etymological dictionary to study words of interest. 6.1 W10

LESSON ONE

MODEL TEXT

- Explain the lesson objective: *to look at personification in a poem.*

- Read the poem aloud. Ask pupils what is being personified. *sleep*

- Spend a moment or two asking pupils to describe what they see in their mind's eye, before looking at particular details.

- Focus on the first four verses, and teach pupils to understand the poem by asking questions about it. Annotate the poem as you discuss it. Ask pupils:

  – Who is the Prince of Sleep? *sleep itself*

  – Why is Sleep 'still and lovely', and why is he in a 'valley steep', a 'lonely place'? *sleep is peaceful, deep like a valley, and you are by yourself, cut off from everyone*

  – How might 'twilight feet' look? And why no sandals? *misty/faded; bare feet are quiet*

  – Which words and phrases in the fourth verse add to the soft effect of the poem? *'phantom', 'misty', 'muffled'*

Word and sentence level work

1 Explore the poetic language: *'eve', 'garb', 'gloomed', 'phantom', 'witch'* (bewitch). With pupils, use a good dictionary to look up their changed meanings – some dictionaries may denote them as 'archaic', 'literary' or 'poetic' words.

2 Underline examples of alliteration and onomatopoeia – all adding to the soft effect: *lovely/lonely; garb/grey; faint/flame; gloomed; muffled;* and long vowel sounds such as *ee, oo, a.*

Group activities: differentiation

Working independently, **lower attainers** complete question 1 using **PCM 9**. **Higher attainers** complete question 2 using **PCM 10**.

Guided reading. Look at verses 5 and 6 in detail.

Plenary

Display the sketches of the Prince of Sleep. Look for similarities and differences. How accurate are the details in relation to the descriptions in the poem?

YOU WILL NEED

- **Pupil's Book** pages 16–17
- **OHT 7** – First four verses
- **PCM 9** – Outline of Sleep
- **PCM 10** – Verses 5 and 6
- **PCM 11** – Homework

 ICT For activities linked to this lesson see **PAGE 103**

HOMEWORK

Ask pupils to think about what the personification of Night might be like. Ask them to make notes on **PCM 11** to prepare for the next lesson.

Link to reading objectives

- To articulate personal responses to literature.   6.1 T3
- To contribute to shared discussion about literature.   6.1 T5

Assumed prior knowledge

- Familiarity with poetry that describes the natural world.
- Metaphor and simile.

Planning suggestion

You can use this unit as part of a week looking at **personification in poetry.** You could look at 'Silver' by Walter de la Mare and 'Bully Night' by Roger McGough.

LESSON TWO

YOU WILL NEED

- **OHT 8** – Night
- **PCM 12** – Writing frame
- **Prompt Chart 3** – Similie and metaphor

WRITING

- Recap the work done in the previous lesson and discuss how Walter de la Mare used peaceful associations of sleep for his personification.

- Explain the lesson objective: *to write a poem which personifies Night.*

- Ask pupils to feedback some of the ideas from their homework notes. Start by asking about the feelings they associate with night.

- Discuss the different people Night could be: *male or female? a plump cosy grandmother? a sinister sneaky thief?*

- Build up a picture of what night might look like. Ask pupils to contribute ideas. Emphasise that there is no one correct response – it is much more interesting if people choose differently.

- Scribe some key words and phrases opposite each question by asking for more precise detail of colour/texture/smell/sound. Encourage pupils to choose 'poetic' words, and examples of onomatopoeia and alliteration.

- Combine some of the details with the 'people' the children have suggested to create a personified description. Write one or two lines for each description.

Group activities: Differentiation

Pupils write their own 'Night' poem. Emphasise that they are not aiming at a rhyming poem. They should put each new idea/image on a new line, and choose strong verbs and vivid adjectives. You may wish to display the **Prompt Chart** to remind them about similie and metaphor.

Lower attainers can use the writing frame on **PCM 12** for support.

Guided writing. Help pupils to find words with the exact shade of meaning they want. Work on alliterative and onomatopoaeic effects.

 For activities linked to this lesson see **PAGE 103**

Plenary

Read some of the work in progress. Pick out examples of effective personification or of poetic words and phrases, onomatopoaeia and alliteration.

WATCH OUT FOR

- ▶ Irrelevant description which does not develop the personification.
- ▶ Inappropriate attempts to use rhyme.

EXTENDED WRITING

Pupils revise their poems and write a final draft to read aloud in a future lesson.

6

Beowulf ● SCREENPLAY

MAIN WRITING OBJECTIVE

- **To prepare a short section of a story as a script.** 6.1 T9

Word and sentence level objectives

- To understand complex sentences and sophisticated punctuation. 6.1 S5 S6
- To revise word classes. 6.1 S1

LESSON ONE

MODEL TEXT

YOU WILL NEED
- **Pupil's Book** pages 19–20
- **OHT 9** – Extract
- **PCM 13** – Film ideas

- Explain the lesson objective: *to look at the dramatic effect of a piece of literature.*

- Give pupils a brief introduction to Beowulf, the Anglo-Saxon hero who fought the evil Grendel and his avenging mother. This extract comes from near the end of the story. Beowulf is now King of the Geats and quite an old man. He is about to meet his last challenge.

- Read the extract aloud, with plenty of dramatic expression.

- Re-read the description of what the slave saw in the cave (paragraph 2). Ask pupils to describe what they see in their minds' eye, using clues from the text.

- What would the slave do or say when he arrived at Beowulf's hall? Why isn't that part included? *would explain to Beowulf what had happened; not included because we know this from narrative and it would interrupt dramatic flow*

Word and sentence level work

1 Look at the second sentence of paragraph 3. Point out the different clauses and connectives used. Turn it into several short sentences: e.g. *He lifted up a gold goblet. He picked his way past the dragon. He made his way out of the cave. He ran over the moor to Beowulf's hall.* Discuss what effect this has. *less dramatic, no emotion*

2 Look at how short sentences are used for dramatic effect: e.g. *The slave was terrified. The dragon took revenge.*

3 Underline examples of vivid adjectives and strong verbs which bring the scene alive.

Group activities: differentiation

All pupils complete both questions. You may prefer them to work in pairs. **Lower attainers** can use **PCM 13** for support.

Guided reading. Work with **high attainers** to explore sentence structure in more detail. Look at the variety of sentences in paragraphs 4 and 5.

Plenary

Ask pupils to read their summaries and describe what they would include in a film of *Beowulf*.

ICT For activities linked to this lesson see **PAGE 103**

ICT For activities linked to this lesson see **PAGE 103**

HOMEWORK

Ask pupils to draw three sketches to show their ideas for the opening scene, the dragon's cave, and the burning stronghold. If possible, encourage them to do some research to find out what clothes Beowulf would wear.

Link to reading objective

- To articulate a personal response to literature.   6.1 T3

Assumed prior knowledge

- Playscripts.   5.1 T18
- Familiarity with storyboarding and film terminology.

Planning suggestion

You could use this unit to form part of a week comparing stories and scripts, or you could focus on *Beowulf* and other classic poems. You could compare this extract with Rosemary Sutcliffe's *Beowulf*.

LESSON TWO

WRITING

- Explain the lesson objective: *to make a short film script using the Beowulf story.*

- Discuss whether the story would work best as an animated film or a film with real actors. Ask pupils to give reasons for their choice.

 • Recap the main settings: the wild moor, the dragon's cave, Beowulf's stronghold.

- Recap the events: the slave finding the treasure, the dragon setting fire to the stronghold, Beowulf calling a meeting. Add these notes to the planning sheet.

 • Demonstrate how to use the screenplay writing frame. Discuss what you might show in the first scene and what shots you might use: e.g. *a long shot to establish the setting, then long panning shot sweeping across the moor to the headland, then zoom in to caves.*

- Make brief notes for scene two to describe the action or sound effects.

- Using pupils' suggestions, model writing a couple of lines of film dialogue for scene three. Explain that the dialogue needs to be speech you would expect to hear in a film – it does not need to be literary language or full sentences.

Group activities: differentiation

In pairs, pupils use the notes from shared writing to help them plan the screenplay for the first three scenes (**PCM 14**).

Lower attaining pupils may cope better with the storyboard on **PCM 15** and perhaps just one or two scenes.

Guided writing. Help pupils to choose key moments for each scene and to word the dialogue appropriately.

Plenary

Choose some pupils to present their plans so far and to explain what they intend to do next.

EXTENDED WRITING

Pupils write their screenplays, including more detailed storyboards for the different scenes.

YOU WILL NEED

- **OHT 10** – Planning sheet
- **OHT 11** – Screenplay writing frame
- **PCM 14** – Screenplay writing frame
- **PCM 15** – Storyboard

 ICT For activities linked to this lesson see **PAGE 103**

 WATCH OUT FOR

▶ Problems in focusing on key moments.
▶ Inappropriate dialogue.

49

7

In the News • JOURNALISM

MAIN WRITING OBJECTIVE

- **To develop journalistic style.**   6.1 T15
- **To use journalistic style to report on real or imagined events.**   6.1 T16

Word and sentence level objective

- Punctuation marks: colon, semi-colon, parenthetic commas, dashes and brackets.   6.1 S6

LESSON ONE

MODEL TEXT

- Explain the lesson objective: *to identify the features of journalistic writing.*

- Look at the article, and refer briefly to the headline. Ask pupils to predict what the article might be about about.

- Tell pupils you will be looking at how one journalist reported the first round the world balloon journey. The article is based on an interview. Explain that journalists present facts using a particular language and style.

- Read aloud the first three paragraphs of the article. Ask pupils:
  - What question do you think the journalist asked to get information for his first paragraph? *What did you look forward to most, on landing?*
  - Why do you think the journalist started his article with this? *to create immediate human interest*
  - Which details are facts, not arising from the interview? *21 days; 29,000 miles; touch-down time, size of the balloon*
  - Which details are the balloonists' views? *what Jones wanted to do when he landed; best bit was the finishing line*

- Point out examples of direct speech. Explain that speech is a key feature of journalistic writing as it adds variety and real interest to reports.

Word and sentence level work

Underline examples of a semi-colon, colon, and commas used instead of brackets (parenthetic commas). Ask pupils to discuss how and why they are used.

Group activities: differentiation

All pupils read the rest of the article in their books and complete questions 1 and 2. **Higher attainers** can go on to complete the sentences in question 3.

Plenary

1 Ask pupils to feedback their question ideas.

2 Ask pupils to give examples of direct and reported speech.

YOU WILL NEED

- **Pupil's Book** pages 22–23
- **OHT 12** – Article extract
- **PCM 16** – Homework: Newspaper article

ICT For activities linked to this lesson see **PAGE 103**

HOMEWORK

Pupils re-read the story of Beowulf on **PCM 16**, then list some facts and quotations that they can use later as the basis for a newspaper report.

Link to reading objective

- To comment critically on the language, style and success of examples of non-fiction such as periodicals, reviews, reports, leaflets. 6.1 T12

Assumed prior knowledge

- Unit 6 – Beowulf.
- The features of newspapers, including layout and headlines. 4.1 T20
- Use of ICT to draft and lay out reports. 4.1 T24
- Direct and reported speech. 5.1 S5

Planning suggestion

You can use this unit as part of a week looking at **newspaper reports**. Compare the more sensational style and shorter sentences of tabloid journalism with the more formal style of the article in this unit.

LESSON TWO

WRITING

- Explain the lesson objective: *to use journalistic style to report on an event from* Beowulf.

- Using the **Prompt Chart**, re-cap the main features of journalistic writing.

- Ask pupils to share their homework ideas. Make a note of a selection of these on the flipchart, under the headings *Facts* and *Quotations*.

- Brainstorm possible headlines for the report: e.g. *Beowulf Threatens Revenge, Slave finds Dragon's Lair, Dragon Devastates Land.*

- With pupils plan the first paragraph. What will it focus on? Remind them to think of a gripping first sentence. Encourage the use of complex punctuation such as parenthetic commas: e.g. *Today, amid smouldering heaps of ash, Beowulf swore revenge on a deadly dragon.*

- Use some of the suggested quotations to model the use of direct or reported speech, e.g. *At a gathering of warrior Geats, Beowulf said, 'I'll fight this alone'.*

- With the pupils, decide on two or three other paragraph headings.

- Remind pupils that they can use opinions and details of human interest as well as hard facts.

Group activities: differentiation

All pupils attempt the three activities. **Lower attainers** can use the writing frame on **PCM 17** for support.

Guided writing. Support **lower attainers** in writing the first paragraph. Help them to write longer sentences and use complex punctuation.

Plenary

1 Look at pupils' headlines. Discuss interesting puns or catchy phrases.

2 Ask two groups to read aloud their first paragraph. Others comment on style and impact.

EXTENDED WRITING

Pupils complete a first draft of their article and ask a partner to comment on spellings, punctuation and successful journalistic features.

They can then design a layout for the article: headline, size of lettering and typeface, columns, space for pictures.

YOU WILL NEED

- **PCM 16** – Homework: Newspaper article
- Flipchart headed:
  Facts
  Quotations
- **PCM 17** – Writing frame
- **Prompt Chart 4** – Journalistic writing

ICT For activities linked to this lesson see **PAGE 103**

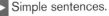

WATCH OUT FOR

- ▶ Simple sentences.
- ▶ Balance of 'facts' and reported views.
- ▶ Difficulty in translating dialogue into reported speech.

8

Summing Up • SCHOOL REPORT

MAIN WRITING OBJECTIVES

• To adopt the distinctive voice of a school report.	6.1 T14
• To summarise a text in a specified number of words.	6.1 T8

Word and sentence level objectives

• To use dictionaries and spell checks.	6.1 W3
• To adapt texts for particular readers and purposes.	6.1 S1
• To investigate connecting words and phrases.	6.1 S4

LESSON ONE

MODEL TEXT

• Explain the lesson objective: *to read and summarise a school report.*

• Briefly discuss the purpose and audience of school reports. What kind of information do they provide? *progress in subjects, exam results, teacher assessments, personal and social development, etc*

• Explain that reports are written in a distinctive style. They should be clear and easy for parents to understand. They should be fair and unprejudiced – mainly giving facts, not opinions. They are mostly written in the present tense and in the third person.

• Look at the extracts from Jane Johnson's school report. Skim read, pointing out the different headings.

• Read aloud the sections for English and Maths. Ask pupils:

– What words might you use to describe Jane's character? *shy, quiet, well-behaved, hard-working*

– What is she good at? *reading aloud, spelling new words, straightforward sums, working in a group*

– What are her weaknesses? *writing slowly, not understanding things, lack of confidence, not joining in discussion*

Word and sentence level work

1 Discuss the use of short sentences and clear punctuation. Explain that this is done so that the meaning is as clear as possible.

2 Point out the logical connective: *consequently.* Look at the connectives which qualify statements: *when, but, although, however.*

Group activities: differentiation

Lower attainers complete question 1, using the extra support provided by **PCM 18. Higher attainers** complete question 2 using **PCM 19.**

Guided reading. Use the text to practise spelling basic 'subject' vocabulary. Make a list of useful words: e.g. *English, technology, science, mathematics, personal and social development.*

Plenary

Read some of the summaries of Jane's general progress. Do they give a clear picture of her?

YOU WILL NEED

• **Pupil's Book** pages 25–26
• **PCM 18** – Summary
• **PCM 19** – General progress

ICT For activities linked to this lesson see **PAGE 103**

HOMEWORK

Display the list of useful subject vocabulary. Ask pupils to learn these spellings. They can add other useful words of their own if they wish.

Link to reading objectives

- To distinguish between fact and opinion.   6.1 T11
- To comment critically on language and style of school reports.   6.1 T12

Assumed prior knowledge

- Personal and impersonal writing.
- Non-chronological reports.   5.2 T22

Planning suggestion

You can use this unit as part of a week looking at fact and opinion.

LESSON TWO

WRITING

YOU WILL NEED

- **OHT 13** – Blank report
- **PCM 20** – School report

- Spend five minutes on paired or shared spelling tests, concentrating on vocabulary for the report.

- Remind pupils of the school report they read yesterday. Reiterate the key points: *short sentences, clear punctuation, present tense, fair, fact not opinion.*

- Explain the lesson objective: *to write their own school report as fairly and honestly as possible.*

- Model the shared writing on yourself or ask a confident pupil to volunteer. With pupils' contributions, complete a few sentences for one subject. Remember to use facts, not opinions, and to make the writing clear and easy to understand.

Group activities: differentiation

All pupils attempt to write their own report using the framework on **PCM 20**. **Lower attainers** may write about a couple of subjects only. If self-conscious or less confident children are uneasy, they may prefer to write about a character from a book they have read.

Guided writing. Help pupils to balance strengths and weaknesses using connectives. Work with **lower attainers** on writing summaries, and encourage pupils who are not particularly academic to focus on their strengths (e.g. they may excel at drawing or PE, or be good with computers).

Plenary

Read out one or two of the reports without revealing the name of the pupil. Can pupils guess whose report it is? Are the reports fair and balanced?

EXTENDED WRITING

Pupils finish the final draft of the report.

ICT For activities linked to this lesson see **PAGE 103**

WATCH OUT FOR
▶ Lack of balance.
▶ Inappropriate language

9

Harriet Tubman ● BIOGRAPHY

MAIN WRITING OBJECTIVE

- **To write a biography, adopting the distinctive voice of a historical character.**   6.1 T14

Word and sentence level objectives

- To form complex sentences.   6.1 S5
- To investigate connecting words and phrases.   6.1 S4

LESSON ONE

MODEL TEXT

- Using the **Prompt Chart** discuss how a biography differs from an autobiography.

- Explain the lesson objective: *to look at a biography of Harriet Tubman.*

- Read the extract aloud. Ask pupils:

  – Why is this piece of writing a biography? *third person; facts about a person's life; opinions of writer – written and inferred*

  – What facts about Harriet Tubman are given in the biography? *facts about her early life; date of escape; her work as an adult*

  – What opinions does the writer express or imply about Harriet Tubman, through her writing? *admiration/sympathy – Harriet was only three years old; a long and dangerous journey; bravely devoted her life*

- Ask pupils to suggest how the first two sentences would be written if this was an autobiography e.g.

  I was born a slave in the year 1820 and lived with my family in a one-roomed shack, where we slept on the bare dirt floor. We belonged to a rich farmer called Edward Brodas.

Word and sentence level work

1 Look at the first sentence. Explain that the first part of the sentence is the main clause. The rest of the sentence is the supporting clause, which adds more information. The connective in this sentence is 'where'.

2 Look for other connectives, *'By the age of...'*, *'but...'*, and discuss how longer sentences add interest and variety.

Group activities: Differentiation

Lower attainers complete question 1 using **PCM 21**.

Higher attainers add details to the timeline on **PCM 22**.

Plenary

Invite pupils to suggest events for inclusion on the timeline. Discuss why certain suggestions may or may not be important.

YOU WILL NEED

- **Pupil's Book** pages 28–29
- **Prompt Chart 2** – Biography and Autobiography
- **PCM 21** – Biography
- **PCM 22** – Blank timeline

ICT For activities linked to this lesson see **PAGE 104**

HOMEWORK

Explain that pupils are going to write a biography of Florence Nightingale. Ask them what they know about her. Give a brief account of her life if necessary.
Ask pupils to make a list of the things they will need to find out about Florence Nightingale before they can write a biography.

Link to reading objective

- To distinguish between biography and autobiography. 6.1 T11

Assumed prior knowledge

- Notemaking: to fillet passages for relevant information. 5.3 T16
- Preparation for reading, by identifying what they know and what they need to find out. 5.2 T16

Planning suggestion

You can make the **lives of famous people** a theme for the week. It would be good to look at a selection of biographies including pop stars, footballers, etc.

LESSON TWO

WRITING

- Explain the lesson objective: *to write a short biography of Florence Nightingale.*

- Explain that pupils are going to write a short biography for inclusion in an encyclopaedia. It will be just a few paragraphs so they will have to carefully select which facts to include.

- Drawing on their homework notes, make a list of the questions to which pupils need answers before they can write the biography.

- From this list, draw out paragraph headings: e.g. *early life and family; early career; the Crimean War; achievements.* Write these on a flipchart to guide their writing.

- Now look at the information on the Florence Nightingale timeline.

- Ask pupils what they would write under the first heading 'early life and family'. *when she was born, that she was named after the place where she was born, that her parents did not want her to be a nurse*

- Compose the opening sentences together.

- Ask pupils what opinions they have of Florence Nightingale. Brainstorm words and phrases they could use in their own writing: *caring, dedicated, hardworking.*

Group activities: Differentiation

All pupils continue writing the biography, based on the timeline (**PCM 23**) and any additional research using information books.

Lower attainers can use the writing frame on **PCM 24** for support.

Guided writing. Ensure that **higher attainers** use a variety of connectives, and can punctuate complex sentences appropriately.

Plenary

Compare the work in progress of two or three pupils. Comment on the use of complex sentences, and the factual information. (You may prefer to do this in a later session using an OHT of one pupil's work.)

EXTENDED WRITING

Pupils exchange their biographies with a partner, and discuss possible improvements. They then write a final draft.

YOU WILL NEED

- **OHT 14** – Nightingale timeline
- **PCM 23** – Nightingale timeline
- Information books about Florence Nightingale
- **PCM 24** – Writing frame

ICT For activities linked to this lesson see **PAGE 104**

WATCH OUT FOR
- Use of present tense.
- Paragraphs with more than one focus.

MAIN WRITING OBJECTIVE

- **To write autobiographically, writing in the role of a historical character (linked to work in history).** 6.1 T14

Word and sentence level objectives

- To revise prepositions. 6.1 S1
- To understand how words and expressions change over time. 6.1 W7

LESSON ONE

MODEL TEXT

- Explain the lesson objective: *to look at autobiographical writing in the form of a diary.*

- Explain that diaries can be very important historical records, because they are first-hand accounts. Samuel Pepys is perhaps the most famous diarist ever. His most famous diary entry is on September 2nd, 1666 – the day of the Great Fire of London.

- Read the extract aloud. Ask pupils:

  – Which words or phrases help you to vividly imagine the scene? *e.g. pigeons burning, the shower of fire-drops, the arch of fire*

  – Why are they are so vivid? *they use senses, focus on tiny details*

  – How do you think Pepys might have felt as he watched London burning? *clues in the text: 'with my heart full of trouble', 'poor people', 'poor pigeons', 'could endure no more', 'horrid', 'it made me weep to see it', 'home with a sad heart'*

Word and sentence level work

1 Investigate how the diary has been written in note form, leaving out words: *'I down to the waterside'*. Find other examples.

2 Look at the many prepositions which add to the effect of rushing everywhere: *down, through, into, from, about.*

3 Underline some of the seventeenth century spellings and ask pupils to compare them with current versions: *mayds, gowne, balconys, staid, ruine.* Deduce two common differences from these examples: *extra 'e' and interchangeable 'i' and 'y'.*

Group activities: differentiation

Lower attainers answer question 1 using **PCM 25**.

Higher attainers compare Pepys' diary with the impersonal account of the Great Fire on **PCM 26**.

Guided reading. Support those pupils who find the text too difficult to read independently, or use any available classroom assistance.

Plenary

Review the qualities which make Pepys' diary so vivid. Read the impersonal account on **PCM 26** and point out the use of the passive voice.

YOU WILL NEED

- **Pupil's Book** pages 31–32
- **OHT 15** – Extract from Pepys' Diary
- **PCM 25** – Sights, sounds and smells
- **PCM 26** – Factual account
- **PCM 27** – Homework

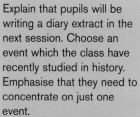

ICT For activities linked to this lesson see **PAGE 104**

HOMEWORK

Explain that pupils will be writing a diary extract in the next session. Choose an event which the class have recently studied in history. Emphasise that they need to concentrate on just one event.

Using **PCM 27**, pupils make background notes about an historical event for diary writing in the next session.

Link to reading objective

- To distinguish between biography and autobiography. 6.1 T11

Assumed prior knowledge

- Personal and impersonal writing.
- General knowledge of the Great Fire of London.

Planning suggestion

You can make **diaries** a theme for the week. You could compare Pepys' diary with Anne Frank's diary or Zlata's diary.

LESSON TWO

YOU WILL NEED

- PCM 28 – Writing frame

WRITING

- Explain the lesson objective: *to imagine that they are witnesses to an important historical event and write a diary entry.*

- Ask pupils to share some of their ideas from the homework activity. Focus on the things they might see, hear, or smell. Start to collect adjectives and nouns to use in the description. If witnessing the Blitz, for example, they might: ***see*** *searchlights, blazing buildings, dark silhouettes;* ***smell*** *smoke, burning;* ***hear*** *sirens, fire engines, people shouting, the crash of falling timbers.* Use present participles and work on precise detail, reminding them of the pigeons in Pepys' account.

- Ask pupils how they would be feeling. Brainstorm some words that would suggest fear or confusion: e.g. *heart thumping, feeling paralysed.*

- Discuss what their personal experience might be. Point out that this is very important because it will make their account unique. Perhaps they lose something that is precious to them? Or see some tiny incident that no one else sees?

- Brainstorm what they might do. How might they end the diary entry for that particular day?

Group activities: differentiation

All pupils draft a diary entry. **Lower attainers** can use the writing frame on **PCM 28** for support. Pupils who still find the task too difficult could write a diary entry for the Great Fire.

Guided writing. Support pupils in using note form and including tiny, specific details. Encourage **higher attainers** to 'live' the experience and use language to express strong feelings through short notes.

For activities linked to this lesson see **PAGE 104**

Plenary

Ask two pupils to read their first drafts and evaluate them. Suggest improvements.

EXTENDED WRITING

Pupils can write further diary entries about the historical event.

WATCH OUT FOR

▶ Slipping out of role.
▶ Difficulties in writing in note form.

Alexander's Story ● STORY WITHIN A STORY

MAIN WRITING OBJECTIVE

- **To use a story within a story to convey the passing of time.** 6.2 T11

Word and sentence level objectives

- To adapt texts for particular purposes. 6.1 S1
- To revise earlier work on verb tenses and to understand the terms active and passive. 6.1 S2
- To revise earlier work on complex sentences. 6.2 S3

LESSON ONE

MODEL TEXT

- Explain that sometimes it is more effective not to tell stories in strict chronological order. In *Beauty and the Beast*, for example, you do not know until the end that the Beast used to be a prince. The story could have started when he was a prince. But then there would not have been a surprise ending.

- Explain the lesson objective: *to look at a story within a story.*

- Read 'Alexander's Story' aloud. Ask pupils:
  - Why do they think the writer did not start the story in 1940? *because it is a ghost story; if he had started in 1940 it would have been much longer and a different kind of story without suspense*

  - In what other ways could the writer have told us what happened to Alexander? *flashbacks, as in a film; perhaps the children could have found Alexander's diary, or looked up the school records and found the story there; perhaps the Head could have told a story within the story*

Word and sentence level work

1 Look for one or two examples of the chatty informal storytelling style: e.g. *contractions, incomplete sentences.*

2 Look at how the verb tenses change through the passage. Pick out examples of past, present and future tenses. Discuss the dramatic effect of using the present tense for Alexander's story – *it makes it feel as if it is happening now.*

Group activities: differentiation

Lower attainers use **PCM 29** to complete question 1. **Higher attainers** complete questions 2 and 3.

Guided reading. Work with **lower attainers** to answer question 3 orally.

Plenary

Recap the rules for using past and present tenses. Ask pupils to give examples.

YOU WILL NEED

- **Pupil's Book** pages 34–35
- **PCM 29** – Verb tenses
- **PCM 30** – Homework

ICT For activities linked to this lesson see **PAGE 104**

HOMEWORK

Pupils think up some ideas for their own ghost story and make brief notes using the planning sheet on **PCM 30**.

- To understand how authors convey the passage of time.   6.2 T1

Assumed prior knowledge

- Verb tenses.
- Ghost stories.

Planning suggestion

You can make **time sequence** a theme for the week, or you could look at other stories which include a story within a story, such as *The Traveller* by Theresa Breslin.

LESSON TWO

WRITING

YOU WILL NEED

- **OHT 16** – Story outline
- **PCM 31** – Planning sheet

- Explain the lesson objective: *to plan and begin to write a story within a story using 'Alexander's Story' as a model.*

- Ask pupils to contribute ideas for a story from their homework notes. Use some of them, explaining why you particularly like them, to build up a shared plot outline.

- Make notes for the first part of the story, which will set the context.

- The second part is the 'story within the story'. Remind pupils that it should have a first person narrator (the ghost). What tense will you use to tell the story within the story? Write the first few sentences together.

- The third part returns to the main story. What tense will you use to tell this part of the story?

- Discuss how the story might end. It needs to have a satisfying resolution to the mystery. Look back at 'Alexander's Story'. Note several possible endings on the OHT.

Group activities: differentiation

In pairs, pupils use their homework notes to plan their own 'story within a story', using the planning sheet on **PCM 31** for support if necessary.

Lower attainers can continue with the work begun in shared writing if they find it helpful.

Guided writing. Concentrate on tenses and building a strong resolution to the story.

ICT For activities linked to this lesson see **PAGE 104**

Plenary

Ask a pair of pupils to present their story outline; the rest of the class can give constructive feedback.

EXTENDED WRITING

Photocopy the planning sheets so that each pupil can continue writing their stories independently. They should also decide on a suitable title. You can use further lessons for pairs to compare versions.

WATCH OUT FOR

▶ Errors in verb tenses.
▶ Difficulty in recognising tense in contractions.
▶ Anti-climax in resolution.

MAIN WRITING OBJECTIVE

- **To write a parody, describing stock characters, plot, language etc.**   6.2 T13

Word and sentence level objective

- To understand how new words have been added to the language.   6.1 W9

LESSON ONE

MODEL TEXT

YOU WILL NEED
- **Pupil's Book** pages 37–38
- **PCM 32** – Extract 2

- Explain the lesson objective: *to identify the typical features of popular horror fiction*.

- Brainstorm a few of the ingredients of popular horror fiction (e.g. *Goosebumps, Point Horror* etc) *characters: exaggerated, larger than life; plot: danger, suspense, things are not what they seem; style: action, dialogue, fast pace*

- Look at the back cover blurb for *Beach Party*. What clues are there that this is a popular horror book? *larger than life characters – 'deliciously dangerous'; threats, danger – 'prepared to kill …'*

- Read the first extract aloud. Ask pupils what typical features it includes. *scary, sinister things happening at night, extreme situations, very 'over the top'*

- Read the second extract aloud. How are these characters typical of popular horror? *exaggerated, trendy, macho, threatening etc*

- Explain that in popular horror, the characters and situations are deliberately exaggerated and a bit over the top. This is done to create a particular dramatic effect. This form of writing is called parody.

Word and sentence level work

1 Study the construction of the first extract: *short paragraphs; short, incomplete sentences – So slimy. So cold. All down her back.* Discuss the dramatic effect of this style of writing.

2 Ask pupils to find new words in the second extract – *surfboard, Day-Glo, boogie etc* and to look them up in a dictionary.

Group activities: differentiation

All pupils complete question 1, using **PCM 32**. **Higher attainers** can go on to question 2.

Guided reading. Work with **higher attainers** to discuss the effect that exaggerated situations, characters and descriptions have on the reader.

Plenary

Ask pupils to contribute ideas for a list of exaggerated features and language used in popular horror. Leave the list displayed.

 For activities linked to this lesson see **PAGE 104**

HOMEWORK

Ask pupils to make notes for a character for their own popular horror story. It could be a hero/heroine or a villain. Remind them to think of exaggerated characteristics, trendy clothes etc.

Link to reading objective

- To identify key features of different types of literary texts, e.g. stock characters, plot structure.   6.2 T7

Assumed prior knowledge

- Understanding of the term 'genre'.

Planning suggestion

You can use this unit as part of a week looking at different genres of fiction, e.g. ghost stories, adventures, school/sport stories, science fiction.

LESSON TWO

WRITING

YOU WILL NEED

- **PCM 33** – Story planner

- Explain the lesson objective: *to write a parody in the popular horror genre*.

- Recap the term 'parody' – an exaggeration of something, a 'take off'. Explain that parodies can be funny because the exaggeration makes them ridiculous.

- Ask pupils to recap the features of popular horror – explain that this genre is a form of parody.

- Ask one or two pupils to describe the typical characters they invented for homework.

- Brainstorm ideas for a plot involving one or more of these characters. Ask pupils to think of exaggerated situations and events. Remember that it should be a bit extreme, even ridiculous, but it is important not to lose sight of the original genre – horror. What happens? Why? Where?

- Brainstorm examples of exaggerated language that could be used in the story: *verbs to describe speech – screamed, yelled, shrieked; verbs describing movement – dragged, stumbled, crept, cowered; adjectives to convey horror – slimy, hideous, grotesque*

- Collect examples of trendy language/slang that could be used in dialogue: *hi, cool, huh, man, guys*

- Together, write a story opening using dialogue.

Group activities: differentiation

PCM 33

All pupils work in mixed ability pairs or groups to support each other. They plan the setting, main characters, plot outline an title for a parody in the popular horror genre.

Guided writing. Help pupils to think of exaggerated events and an opening paragraph using dialogue.

Plenary

Ask some pairs or groups to present their parody outlined. Focus on the need to exaggerate.

EXTENDED WRITING

Pupils continue working in pairs or groups to write their parodies. Evaluate the errectiveness of the exaggeration with a partner,

ICT For activities linked to this lesson see **PAGE 104**

WATCH OUT FOR
- ▶ Difficulty in using exaggerated language.
- ▶ Moving too far from the original.

61

What do you read? • QUESTIONNAIRE

MAIN WRITING OBJECTIVE

- **To discuss how standard English varies in different contexts, e.g. why questionnaires must be specific.** 6.2 T20

Word and sentence level objective

- To understand the features of formal and official language. 6.2 S2

LESSON ONE

YOU WILL NEED

- **Pupil's Book** pages 40–41
- Selection of questionnaires (magazines, consumer products)
- **PCM 34** – Reading questionnaire

MODEL TEXT

- Explain the lesson objective: *to think about the language and purpose of questionnaires.*

- Encourage pupils to describe questionnaires they have seen, and to say what type of information was being sought e.g. *television viewing habits; favourite pop stars; consumer spending; attitudes towards an issue, e.g. drugs, smoking, hunting.* Display some examples if you have any.

PB

- Look at the completed questionnaire. Ask pupils:
  - Who do you think this questionnaire was designed for? *children*
  - How do you know? *refers to teacher and parents*
  - What is its purpose? *to find out about children's reading habits.*
  - What do we know about this person's reading habits? *she likes stories about children at home and school, chooses by reading a bit of the story, enjoys reading at home more than at school*

- Discuss how the questionnaire is set out: *tick boxes, multiple choice answers with space for 'other', questions with written answers.*

- Ask pupils why they think the layout is important. *It makes it quick and easy for people to understand and fill in.*

Word and sentence level work

PB

Discuss the language used in writing questionnaires. Explain that it is very precise and clear. Ask pupils why this is so important. *so people know exactly what information you want; so you get the right answers to the questions*

Group activities: differentiation

PCM 34

All pupils answer both questions using **PCM 34** for question 2.

Guided reading. Support pupils who have difficulty in reading the text, by reading the questions aloud and asking pupils to fill in their responses.

Plenary

Ask pupils what type of person might have written this questionnaire. Why do pupils think these people would be interested in the information?

ICT For activities linked to this lesson see **PAGE 105**

HOMEWORK

Ask pupils to make a list of all the magazines and comics they know of that are read by children of their own age.

Link to reading objective

- To read and understand examples of official language and its characteristic features.   6.2 T17

Assumed prior knowledge

- To collect information and present in a simple format, e.g. wall chart.   4.2 T23
- To use ICT to plan, revise, edit and publish.   6.1 T18

Planning suggestion

You can use this unit as part of a week of looking at **questionnaires**, their language and purpose. Focus on completing and composing questionnaires before looking at how to collate information from them.

LESSON TWO

WRITING

- Explain the lesson objective: *to plan a questionnaire about reading habits.*

- Tell pupils that they will be carrying out a survey of 9–11 year olds to find out which magazines and comics are preferred and why.

- Brainstorm the information you want to find out and the questions you will need to ask. *What attracts children to a particular magazine or comic? Which is the most popular and why?*

- Brainstorm possible answers to the questions: e.g. *What makes you buy a magazine? title; cost; readership; subject matter; content.*

- With pupils plan the first question. Emphasise that the wording of the questions must be unambiguous and precise: e.g. *Which magazine or comic do you like best?*

- The first question could be multiple choice. Ask pupils to suggest examples of comics and magazines read by their age group. Select about six and write these under the question. Explain that it is best to also add 'other' to a multiple choice answer so that people can give a different answer if preferred.

- Discuss how some of the questions might be answered: e.g. *tick boxes, yes/no, comment.* Model possible layouts.

Group activities: differentiation

All pupils work in mixed ability groups to plan three more questions for the questionnaire. Choose a scribe for each group.

Guided writing. Work on clarity of layout and questioning.

Plenary

Ask two groups to present their work in progress, and to explain what information they want from each question.

Other pupils should evaluate the clarity of their questions and the suitability of multiple choice responses.

EXTENDED WRITING

Pupils finish their questionnaires. Circulate the final questionnaires to another class to complete.

YOU WILL NEED

- Selection of questionnaires
- Blank OHT or flipchart

ICT For activities linked to this lesson see **PAGE 105**

WATCH OUT FOR

▶ Ambiguous questions.
▶ Confusing layout.

MAIN WRITING OBJECTIVE

- **To write a balanced report of a controversial issue.**   6.2 T19

Word and sentence level objective

- To build a bank of useful terms and phrases for argument.   6.2 W8

LESSON ONE

YOU WILL NEED

- **Pupil's Book** pages 43–44
- **PCM 35** – For and against
- **PCM 36** – Homework

MODEL TEXT

- Explain the lesson objective: *to identify the features of a balanced written argument.*

- Read aloud the report on zoos. Ask pupils:
    - What is the purpose of the report? *sets out both sides of the argument for and against zoos*
    - What do we learn from the first paragraph? *the topic being discussed*
    - What three main questions does the report discuss? *Is the confinement of animals cruel? Do zoos have an educational role? Can zoos save animals in danger of extinction?*
    - Can you find an argument against the keeping of wild animals in zoos? *animals stressed, bored and frustrated*
    - What is the opposite of this view (the counter-argument)? *animals safer, and can live and breed in peace*

- Explain that although this report uses persuasive language from both sides of the argument, the writer is not trying to persuade anyone to one point of view. It is a balanced report.

Word and sentence level work

1 Ask pupils to identify the persuasive language used in each paragraph. List the words and phrases: e.g. *deprived of their freedom; live in peace.*

2 Brainstorm other persuasive phrases that you could use – for and against zoos.

ICT For activities linked to this lesson see **PAGE 105**

Group activities: differentiation

All pupils complete question 1 using **PCM 35**. **Lower attainers** can make notes on the first section, 'Cruel Confinement?' only.

All pupils complete question 2, expressing their own opinion about zoos.

Plenary

Ask several pupils to read aloud their completed sentence. Discuss the views they express.

HOMEWORK

Introduce a controversial issue of interest to pupils.

Pupils should think carefully about the points for and against the issue. Encourage them to talk with other people about it.

For homework, pupils make notes on **PCM 36**, expressing ideas for and against.

Link to reading objective	
● To identify the features of a balanced argument.	6.2 T16

Assumed prior knowledge	
● The terms fact and opinion.	4.1 T19
● Persuasive words and phrases.	5.3 T15
● Ability to construct an argument in note form and complete text.	5.3 T19

Planning suggestion

You can make **controversy** a theme for the week. Hold a class debate about a current issue that children feel strongly about. Pupils can then write a balanced report on the subject. This unit can also be linked to Unit 22.

LESSON TWO

WRITING

- Spend ten minutes sharing pupils' homework ideas. Make notes on the flipchart under the headings *For* and *Against*. Try to get an equal number of points.

- Use the **Prompt Chart** to recap the features of a balanced report.

- Explain the lesson objective: *to write a balanced report of a controversial issue.*

- Brainstorm a catchy title for the report.

- Using pupils' suggestions, begin to plan the report. Make notes under each section. Model thinking through the argument aloud as you write.

- With pupils, write a short introductory paragraph. Remind them that it should summarise both sides of the argument.

Group activities: differentiation

In pairs, pupils draft paragraph 2 of the report. **Lower attainers** can use PCM 37 for support.

Higher attainers can go on to draft the next paragraph.

Guided writing. Work with **higher attainers** to reinforce the language of argument.

Plenary

Invite two pupils to read their work in progress. Comment on clarity and effectiveness. Invite two other pupils to share their work in progress and discuss which features from the **Prompt Chart** were included.

EXTENDED WRITING

Pupils draft the remaining paragraphs of their report.

They then revise the report and add an introductory paragraph – their own or the one from shared writing.

YOU WILL NEED

- Flipchart with headings *For* and *Against*
- **Prompt Chart 5** – Balanced report
- **OHT 17** – Planning frame
- **PCM 37** – Writing frame

WATCH OUT FOR
- Over-wordy first and last paragraphs.
- Lack of structure in paragraphs.
- Bias.

15 Island of Horror ● ADVENTURE GAME BOOK

MAIN WRITING OBJECTIVE

- **To write in a chosen genre, revising and redrafting to presentational standard.** 6.2 T12

Word and sentence level objective

- To revise the language of instructions and directions. 6.3 S1

LESSON ONE

YOU WILL NEED

- **Pupil's Book** pages 46–47
- **PCM 38** – Headland
- **PCM 39** – Lighthouse
- **PCM 40** – Homework

MODEL TEXT

- Explain the lesson objective: *to analyse the adventure game genre and plan a continuation of the extract.*

- Introduce the basic features of adventure game books. At each stage in the story, the reader has to decide what to do. You turn to different pages of the text to find out what your decision leads to. This genre suits a plot with plenty of action and weird and wonderful settings. It is generally used for fantasy stories.

- Read aloud the 'Your task' section of the extract. Ask pupils:
  - How does this introduction grab your attention? *written as if it is happening now; you are right in the middle of the adventure*
  - Why do you think the writer includes the score-keeping idea? *adds to the 'game' atmosphere and sense of participation*

- Look at the next extract, which comes from the middle of the book. Discuss a few ideas for what you might find at the headland or the old lighthouse. Use the cover illustration for clues. Emphasise the key features of the genre. *action, problems to solve, monsters to fight, clues to find etc.*

Word and sentence level work

1 Ask pupils why the text is written in the present tense. *It makes it feel as if it is happening now, and as if you are part of a real adventure.*

2 Ask pupils to find examples of instructions, using imperative verbs: e.g. *turn to page..., be careful....*

3 Discuss why the text is very simple, without visually descriptive words and phrases. *partly because the pictures do that, but also so you can imagine things for yourself*

Group activities: differentiation

All pupils answer question 1 using **PCM 38**.

Higher attainers produce ideas for a second page on **PCM 39**.

Plenary

Share ideas and evaluate. Have pupils remembered the key features of the genre? Have pupils included two new choices?

ICT For activities linked to this lesson see **PAGE 105**

HOMEWORK

Using **PCM 40**, pupils make notes of some grisly ideas for an adventure game book called *The House of Horrors.*

Link to reading objective

- To identify key features in adventure game texts.　　6.2 T7

Assumed prior knowledge

- Use of imperative tense in instructions.　　5.1 S9
- To discuss, proof-read and edit own writing.　　5.1 S3
- Planning, drafting and revising narrative.

Planning suggestion

You can make **science fiction and fantasy** a theme for the week, using adventure game books as the chosen genre. Pupils can be encouraged to write their own descriptions of fantasy worlds.

LESSON TWO

WRITING

YOU WILL NEED
- **OHT 18** – Flow Chart
- **PCM 41** – Flow chart

- Explain the lesson objective: *to write a new adventure game book called* The House of Horrors.

- Share some of the ideas from pupils' homework and make notes.

- Display the flow chart and explain how it can help with planning an adventure game book.

- With pupils, fill in a brief description of what they will encounter when they go in the back and front doors. Remind pupils about the use of the imperative, and to include options for what to do next.

- Explain that pupils are going to work in groups to plan an adventure game book using a flow chart. Groups must agree on their plan, and then each pupil will contribute a different page.

- You might suggest that the game can be made harder by making most of the decisions in the last row of boxes lead to doom!

  (NB classes that find it difficult to work collaboratively could complete the flow chart outline in shared writing, then work on the pages in pairs.)

Group activities: differentiation

All pupils work in groups to plan, write and illustrate *The House of Horrors* using **PCM 41** to help them. Support comes from working as a whole group. Make sure they agree their flowchart in the first ten minutes.

Guided writing. Help groups to work to an effective plan, and to use the correct verb tenses.

Plenary

Share work in progress. Discuss how to number the pages so that the story sequence is disguised.

 ICT For activities linked to this lesson see **PAGE 105**

EXTENDED WRITING

Pupils can continue with *The House of Horrors* over several lessons. Encourage them to add puzzle ideas and a scoring system as in *The Island of Horrors*. Ask them to write an introduction: 'Your Task'.

WATCH OUT FOR
▸ Inconsistent use of present tense.
▸ Planning difficulties.

● CONVERSATION POEMS

MAIN WRITING OBJECTIVE

● **To use different genres as models to write.**   6.2 T10

Word and sentence level objective

● To revise the setting out of dialogue.

LESSON ONE

MODEL TEXT

● Explain the lesson objective: *to look at examples of conversation poems.*

● Read aloud the three poems. You could ask different pupils to read different parts. Remind them to read expressively – emphasising the mood and meaning by varying the way they speak.

● Ask pupils:

  – Can you identify what the poems have in common? *all have questions in them; all are based on conversations*

  – How do you think Michael Rosen and Karen Jackson got the ideas for their conversation poems? *based on things that had happened to them*

  – In the 'Question and Answer Poem', does it matter whether the answers the children give to their questions are true? Why not? *They are showing wonder at things we do not understand and using their imagination to create magical possibilities.*

● Discuss the mood of each poem. Is it the same mood throughout?

● Discuss the feelings of the characters in each poem.

Word and sentence level work

Use the poems to revise how dialogue is usually set out, i.e. using speech marks and 'said'. Discuss how the dialogue is set out differently in each of these poems. With the pupils, try rewriting a verse of 'Going Through the Old Photos' using speech marks and words such as 'said'. What effect does this have.

Group activities: differentiation

All pupils work in mixed ability groups to discuss and compare two of the poems using **PCM 42**.

Guided reading. Help less fluent readers to understand the difference between mood and feelings.

Plenary

Ask pupils to refer to parts of each poem which convey mood or feelings. Did everyone have the same answers? If not, why not?

YOU WILL NEED

● **Pupil's Book** pages 49–50
● **OHT 19** – Dialogue
● **PCM 42** – Comparing poems: moods and feelings
● **PCM 43** – Homework

ICT For activities linked to this lesson see **PAGE 105**

HOMEWORK

Remind pupils of how a playscript is set out, i.e. character name, directions, no speech marks. Ask them to change the poem, *All for an Ice Cream*, into a short playscript using **PCM 43**.

Link to reading objective

- To understand how messages, moods, feelings and attitudes are conveyed in poetry.   6.2 T5

Assumed prior knowledge

- How to perform poems in different ways.   5.2 T5
- How to analyse and compare poetic styles.   5.1 T7
- Awareness of conventions of playscripts.   5.1 T18

Planning suggestion

You can make **conversation poetry** a theme for the week. Look at the different ways in which dialogue can be presented and turned into poetry. Encourage pupils to write and perform their own poems.

LESSON TWO

WRITING

- Explain the lesson objective: *to write a 'question and answer' poem about the weather.*

- Re-read the 'Question and Answer Poem' and use it as a model for shared writing.

- Start by listing several questions about the weather on a blank OHT or flipchart: e.g. *What is thunder? Why does it rain? What are hailstones? Where does the wind go? What is fog?*

- Ask pupils to think of interesting and imaginative responses e.g.

  – What is Thunder?

  Boulders rolling down a steep hill.

  Horses stampeding across the plains.

  A giant strolling through the woods.

- Remind them to think about conveying mood and feeling.

- Decide which 'answer' will be the second line of the poem.

  – What is Thunder?

  A giant strolling through the woods

- Choose another question from the list to be line 3. Make a note of pupils' responses and select one response to be line 4 of the poem.

Group activities: differentiation

All pupils work independently to write their own 'question and answer' Weather Poems.

Lower attainers can use the questions from shared writing.

Guided writing. Work with **higher attainers** to help them plan questions and write metaphors into the responses.

Plenary

Invite pupils to share their poems.

EXTENDED WRITING

Pupils swap poems with a partner, revise their work and produce a neat copy for a class anthology.

YOU WILL NEED
- **Pupil's Book** page 50.
- A flipchart or blank OHT

ICT For activities linked to this lesson see **PAGE 105**

WATCH OUT FOR
- Lack of relationship between question and answer.
- Abrupt change of mood.

MAIN WRITING OBJECTIVES

- **To discuss how standard English varies in different contexts.**   6.2 T20
- **To anticipate possible objections to arguments.**   6.2 T18

Word and sentence level objectives

- To understand the features of formal and official language.   6.2 S2
- To investigate active and passive verbs.   6.2 S1

LESSON ONE

MODEL TEXT

- Explain the lesson objective: *to consider the features, audience and purpose of public notices.*

- Everywhere we go we are bombarded with print. Briefly brainstorm some of the main kinds of writing you may see in a typical street – advertisements, directions, road names, warning notices, shop signs etc. You could display some photographs of your local area.

- Sometimes notices can be very important, and must be easy to see and read. Ask pupils to suggest some examples: *e.g. warning signs, directions on a road.*

- Some public notices tell us things we need to know: *e.g. rules we must keep, changes that are planned, or dangers we might meet.*

- Look at some of the notices on the OHT and ask pupils where they would be likely to see them. Which ones:
  a) instruct or warn you about something?
  b) inform you about something?
  c) try to persuade you ?

Word and sentence level work

- Find examples of passive verbs e.g. *allowed, appreciated*. Ask pupils why they think they are used. *so that it sounds impersonal*

- Find examples of imperative verbs. Notice where 'please' is added. Ask pupils what effect this has.

- Discuss how the layout and style of print or handwriting affects your reaction to the notices.

Group activities: differentiation

In pairs, pupils read and discuss the notices in the **Pupil's Book**.

Lower attainers can focus on just a few examples.

Guided reading. Look at the langue of the notices and how this affects the tone.

Plenary

Ask pairs of pupils to explain their notes. Discuss the effect of language, layout, etc. on the reader's reaction.

YOU WILL NEED

- **Pupil's Book** pages 52–54
- Photographs of local area, showing street signs (optional)
- **OHT 20** – Notices

ICT For activities linked to this lesson see **PAGE 106**

HOMEWORK

Ask pupils to look out for some examples of public notices and copy them.

Link to reading objective	
● To read and understand examples of official language.	6.2 T17

Assumed prior knowledge	
● General awareness of notices, signs and labels.	
● Features of instructions; imperative verbs.	4.1 T22

Planning suggestion

You can use this unit as the basis for a week of looking at and classifying further examples of **environmental print**.

LESSON TWO

WRITING

- Display the notices you have collected from around the school and ask pupils to evaluate them. How effective are they? How easy are they to read and understand? How might they be improved? Look at the examples the pupils have brought in.

- Explain the lesson objective: *to compose notices for the school.*

- Brainstorm possible subjects: e.g. *tidiness, health and safety, school organisation.* Discuss the places around school where it might be appropriate to display them.

- Choose one of the subjects and discuss what type of notice would be appropriate: e.g. *instructions; information; rules; persuasion.*

- Ask pupils:

  – What sort of language will you use?

  – What format should it have? Hand-written/word-processed/black and white or colour?

- With pupils, draft the notice. As you write remember to use some of the features discussed in the previous session. Refer to **Prompt Chart 6.**

Group activities: differentiation

In pairs, pupils produce a notice for school. Differentiation will be by outcome.

Guided writing. Work on economy of expression and tone of voice.

Plenary

Evaluate work in progress against the features on **Prompt Chart 6.** Discuss where the notices might go – explain that you have to get permission before putting up a notice, in school or elsewhere.

EXTENDED WRITING

Pupils continue to work on their notices, producing final copies that can be displayed around the school.

YOU WILL NEED

- Examples of notices displayed around the school
- **Prompt Chart 6** – Public Notices

 ICT For activities linked to this lesson see **PAGE 106**

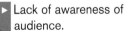 **WATCH OUT FOR**

▶ Lack of awareness of audience.
▶ Difficulty in adopting appropriate tone and language – too informal or impolite.

MAIN WRITING OBJECTIVE

- To produce an extended piece of writing in one genre for a class anthology. 6.2 T12

Word and sentence level objective

- To revise work on editing. 6.2 S4

LESSON ONE

MODEL TEXT

NOTE: If pupils are unsure about haiku it will be worth spending some time refreshing their memory before working on this unit.

- Explain the lesson objective: *to look at examples of tankas.*

- A tanka is a Japanese poem of five lines. It is based on the haiku but with two extra lines. The original custom in Japan was that when someone sent you a haiku you added the two lines as your reply. Nowadays tankas are written as complete poems. The syllables for each line are 5, 7, 5, 7, 7, making 31 syllables altogether. As in haiku, every word counts, so you have to choose them carefully.

- Read aloud 'Singing'. Mark the OHT as you ask pupils:
  – What is 'Singing' describing? *someone singing a song which people remember and will perhaps whistle later on*
  – Why do you think it says 'my' song? *perhaps the poet is the composer or perhaps he was singing the song and it feels personal to him*

- Count the syllables of each line – 5, 7, 5, 7, 7. Show the divisions clearly by marking them on the OHT.

Word and sentence level work

This is incorporated in the writing activities in Lesson Two.

Group activities: differentiation

Lower attainers who have difficulty in counting syllables, complete question 1 using **PCM 44**.

Higher attainers read the haiku on **PCM 45** and change two of them into tanka. This can be completed for homework.

Plenary

Ask some pupils to read their tanka aloud. Have they used the right number of syllables? Does every word deserve its place? Discuss possible improvements.

YOU WILL NEED

- **Pupil's Book** page 56
- **OHT 21** – Tanka
- **PCM 44** – 'Tree'
- **PCM 45** – Haiku into tanka

 ICT For activities linked to this lesson see **PAGE 106**

HOMEWORK

Pupils can either change more of the haiku on **PCM 45** into tanka or choose a tanka they have already written and make a final copy of it for a class anthology.

Link to reading objective

- To recognise how poets manipulate words.   6.2 T3

Assumed prior knowledge

- Counting syllables.   4.3 T5
- Haiku.   4.3
- Similies and metaphors.

Planning suggestion

You can make **haiku and tanka** a theme for the week, finishing by producing a class anthology of pupils' work.

LESSON TWO

WRITING

- Start by reading aloud some of the homework drafts or finished tanka.

- Explain the lesson objective: *to write a complete tanka.*

- **OHT 21** Show the marked OHT from yesterday to remind pupils of the number of syllables in each line.

- Like haiku, tanka are snapshots which capture a small moment. There is usually a bigger meaning as well. Discuss suitable subjects.

- Model a tanka about the view from the classroom window. Ask pupils to contribute words and phrases to describe what they can see.

- Ask pupils what they notice. How does it make them feel? Pick out significant details.

- Start to model the tanka. Remind pupils of the need to organise the lines into the right number of syllables

- The title is important too. In 'Tree', it is the title that explains who is speaking. Ask pupils to suggest titles for the shared poem. It could be straightforward: 'Classroom Window', or it could be metaphorical: 'Prisoner!'.

YOU WILL NEED

- **OHT 21** – Tanka (marked)
- **PCM 45** – Haiku into Tanka

Group activities: differentiation

PCM 45 **All pupils** write their own tanka. **Lower attainers** can continue to work on **PCM 45** if necessary.

Guided writing. Work with pupils on editing the lines to get the correct number of syllables. You could also write a group poem with lower attainers.

Plenary

Ask some pupils to read their tanka and evaluate them. Do they have the right number of syllables?

EXTENDED WRITING

Pupils can swap their tanka with a partner and evaluate. They can then make any changes and produce a final polished copy for a class anthology.

WATCH OUT FOR
- ▶ Lack of focus.
- ▶ Difficulty in counting syllables.

19

Bun Stew ● NONSENSE POEMS

MAIN WRITING OBJECTIVE

- **To use different genres as models for writing.**　　6.2 T10

Word and sentence level objectives

- To understand conventions of language.　　6.2 S2
- To recognise common letter strings.　　6.2 W3

LESSON ONE

MODEL TEXT

OHT 22
OHT 23

- Explain the lesson objective: *to look at several nonsense poems.*

- Read aloud the poems 'The New Weatherperson's First Appearance' by Ian Serraillier, 'Spellbound' by Norman Vandal, and 'Bun Stew' by Julie Holder.

- Ask pupils what these poems have in common. *they all make words into nonsense by spelling them differently or changing the first letter; you need to see them as well as hear them to get the joke*

- As well as being muddled up, the new words have absurd meanings. Pick out some favourites.

- Try making sense of the weather forecast by reading it 'properly'.

- Do pupils know the children's rhyme, 'One, two buckle my shoe'? Point out that 'Bun Stew' is a nonsense version of this. Ask pupils to point out the words that are the numbers in 'Bun Stew'.

Word and sentence level work

1 Ask pupils to try to think of amusing alternatives for months of the year similar to Flyday: e.g. *Gran-uary, Web-uary, Parch.*

2 Ask pupils to look up Spoonerisms. Share these examples: *I've hissed my mystery lesson; a well-boiled icicle; a half-warmed fish; the Lord is a shoving leopard; he's a boiled sprat.*
Convert them back into standard English.

3 Ask pupils to invent some more.

Group activities: differentiation

PCM 46

All pupils correct the spelling in 'Spellbound' using **PCM 46.**

Higher attainers can go on to invent nonsense days of the week and numbers.

Plenary

Look at pupils' suggestions for days of the week and numbers. Make a list of some of the best ideas for numbers for display during the second lesson.

YOU WILL NEED

- **Pupil's Book** pages 58–59
- **OHT 22** – Weather Person/Spellbound
- **OHT 23** – Bun Stew
- **PCM 46** – Spellbound
- **PCM 47** – Homework

ICT For activities linked to this lesson see **PAGE 106**

HOMEWORK

Pupils find different ways to spell the words on **PCM 47**, then write each of the homophones into a sentence. You may need to remind pupils of the meaning of 'homophone'.

Link to reading objective

● To investigate humourous verse: nonsense words and how meaning can be made of them.   6.2 T4

Assumed prior knowledge

● Some familiarity with humourous verse and word play.

Planning suggestion

You can make **playing with words** a theme for the week. Look at other nonsense poetry, such as 'Jabberwocky' by Lewis Carroll, and nonsense stories such as Michael Rosen's 'Hansel and Gristle'.

LESSON TWO

WRITING

● Explain the lesson objective: *to write a nonsense verse, based on* 'Bun Stew'.
● Explain to pupils that they will be playing around with words and using rhyme.
● Read 'Bun Stew' again. Put brackets round each group of three lines. Underline the 'numbers'. Point out the change in rhythm and the extra line for ten, twelve and twenty.
● Ask pupils to suggest new words for the first few numbers. Emphasise that the new word should sound quite like the 'proper' one but it does not have to rhyme exactly: e.g. *'eleven' and 'elephant'*. They should try to find an absurd word. Use some of the nonsense numbers from the list made in the previous session.
● Compose the first three lines of a new poem together: e.g.
> *Fun do*
> *I joined the queue.*

Be prepared for rude alternatives!

Group activities: differentiation

All pupils work in mixed ability groups to draft a nonsense number poem. Alternatively they can write a 'days of the week' poem.

Lower attainers can use **PCM 48** to help them, and just take the number poem to 5 or 10 rather than 20.

Guided writing. Help pupils to recognise and use partial rhymes.

Plenary

Read some of the poems and evaluate. How successful are they? Suggest any improvements.

EXTENDED WRITING

Pupils can revise and edit their poems and make a final copy to go in a class book of nonsense poems.

YOU WILL NEED

● **OHT 23** – Bun Stew
● **PCM 48** – Number nonsense framework

ICT For activities linked to this lesson see **PAGE 106**

WATCH OUT FOR

▶ Difficulty in using partial rhymes.

20

The Earth Centre

● PUBLIC INFORMATION

MAIN WRITING OBJECTIVES

- **To discuss variations of standard English in different contexts.** 6.2 T20
- **To plan and create a guide book or website.**

Word and sentence level objective

- To understand conventions of public information documents. 6.2 S2

LESSON ONE

MODEL TEXT

- Explain the lesson objective: *to look at the language used in information aimed at the public.*

- Give pupils two minutes to get an overview of **The Earth Centre** material in their books. Ask them where they think this information might have come from. List their suggestions, and stress the link between the website page and the other extracts.

- Look at the first page of the leaflet in detail. Ask pupils:

  – What is special about this text? *aimed directly at the reader, persuasive, varied in size, eye-catching*

  – What facts are included on this page? *400 acres, South Yorkshire.*

  – Which words show personal opinions? *beautiful, interesting, exciting, innovative*

  – What words are used to excite and spur the reader into action? *relax, explore, play, enjoy, experience*

  Point out that these are all imperative verbs.

Word and sentence level work

1 Scan the extracts for examples of imperatives at the beginning of sentences: *'Hunt it out', 'Be amazed', 'Take your shoes off'.* Underline them on the OHT.

2 Find examples of an imperative in the middle of a sentence: *discover its ... , feel the textures... , listen to the sounds....* Underline them on the OHT.

3 Compile a list of imperatives, which give an order: e.g. *Be quiet!*

Group activities: differentiation

All pupils complete questions 1 and 2, writing a 'Fred says' caption and drawing a sketch of what they would expect to do in NatureWorks.
Higher attainers complete question 3.

Plenary

Invite two pupils to read their 'Fred Says' captions. With the rest of the class, comment on their use of language.

Note pupils' ideas about how **The Earth Centre** got its name.

YOU WILL NEED

- **Pupil's Book** pages 61–63
- **OHT 24** – first page of leaflet
- **OHT 25** – inside the guide
- **PCM 49** – Homework

 ICT For activities linked to this lesson see **PAGE 106**

HOMEWORK

Pupils complete **PCM 49**, rewriting what 'Fred says' as a guide book or website entry. Remind them to use persuasive language and imperatives.
Lower attainers could complete only part of the activity.

Link to reading objective

- To read and understand examples of official language, e.g. consumer information documents.   6.2 T17

Assumed prior knowledge

- Use ICT to plan, revise and publish.   6.1 T18
- Imperative verbs.   5.1 S9
- How to design an advert using features from reading.   4.3 T25
- Familiarity with information leaflets.

Planning suggestion

You can make **public information leaflets and guides** a theme for the week. If possible, compare the printed form with information websites

LESSON TWO

WRITING

- Explain the lesson objective: *to plan and create a guide in the form of a leaflet or pages of a website.*

- Explain that pupils are going to write it in the style of **The Earth Centre** guide. How it is planned and written will depend on the subject and who it is written for.

- Agree on the subject of the guide: a place, or event, which all the class know well. Choose something pupils feel enthusiastic about.

- Now agree an audience: *e.g. school children, local families or the general public.*

- Think of a catchy phrase or slogan for the front page of the guide.

- Brainstorm all the things you would like to include. Explain that some of these will be useful headings for entries in their guide.

- Choose one of the headings. With pupils, make notes of facts and opinions about it (possibly as a word-web).

- Pupils turn this into a leaflet or a website page, modelled on **The Earth Centre** extract. Encourage pupils to be enthusiastic – however ordinary the item. You could have 'Fred says' style facts as well as lively and persuasive text.

Group activities: differentiation

In pairs, pupils plan and write an entry for the guide. **Higher attainers** should also revise it and write a further entry.

Guided writing. Ensure that all pairs understand the use of the imperative in persuading and inviting others.

Plenary

Ask two pairs of pupils to read out their entries. Evaluate and comment on good examples of persuasive language.

EXTENDED WRITING

Pupils continue planning and writing their guide, including a full list of all the attractions.

Ask pupils to design the layout and illustration carefully, based on a guide or website page they have seen.

YOU WILL NEED

- Collection of guide books
- Website pages

 ICT For activities linked to this lesson see **PAGE 106**

 WATCH OUT FOR
▶ Over-long sentences.
▶ Lack of awareness of audience.

● PARAGRAPHS AND ENDINGS

MAIN WRITING OBJECTIVES

- **To use different genres as models for writing.**   6.2 T10
- **To understand links between paragraphs.**   6.3 T21

Word and sentence level objective

- To revise complex sentences and clauses.   6.2 S3

LESSON ONE

YOU WILL NEED

- **Pupil's Book** pages 65–66
- **OHT 26** – Alone in the mountains
- **PCM 50** – Butch's feelings
- **PCM 51** – Homework
- **Prompt Chart 7** – Paragraphs

MODEL TEXT

- Explain the lesson objective: *to look at how a text is organised into paragraphs, and how each paragraph gives us a bit more information.*

- Use **Prompt Chart 7** to discuss the function of paragraphs.

- Read aloud the first four paragraphs of the extract. Ask pupils:

   – What does the first paragraph tell us about how Butch is feeling? *confused, unsure, unhappy and frightened*

   – What might Butch be thinking in paragraph 2? *the others have left me; I'm scared of going back alone*

   – How does paragraph 2 link with Butch's feelings in paragraph 1? *explains why he is uneasy and unhappy*

   – How does paragraph 3 connect to paragraph 2? *contradicts his initial feelings; explains what is really going on*

   – Look at how paragraph 4 moves the action on, increases the pace of the story and adds suspense.

Word and sentence level work

1 Focus on the complex sentences in paragraph 2. Explain that each sentence has a main clause which tells you what is happening, and subordinate clauses which add detail.

2 Underline the main clause in the first sentence: *'He sat up.'* Point out that it makes sense on its own. Underline the subordinate clauses in another colour: e.g. *'realised quickly enough ...'*, *'but couldn't understand the gloom'*.

3 Scan the text to find examples of words which connect clauses: e.g. *'and'*, *'but'*, *'because'*.

 ICT   For activities linked to this lesson see **PAGE 107**

Group activities: differentiation

All pupils attempt both questions, using **PCM 50** for question 2.

Lower attainers can be asked to complete just part one, or support them to complete the whole in guided group work.

Plenary

For each extract on **PCM 50**, discuss what Butch might have been thinking. Ask pupils to justify their ideas.

HOMEWORK

1 Pupils look at the summaries of the last three paragraphs on **PCM 51**, and write their own ideas about how each incident might have affected Butch. How did he feel or what did he think?

2 Ask them to make notes on how they would want the story to end. They write what Butch might be thinking in the right hand column.

Link to reading objective

- To analyse how individual paragraphs are structured in writing,
  e.g. follow shifting thoughts of a character.   6.2 T2

Assumed prior knowledge

- Planning narrative structure.   6.1 T7
- Identifying the narrator.   6.1 T2
- Understanding links between paragraphs.   5.1 T14

Planning suggestion

You can use **story endings** as a theme for the week, with pupils planning, revising and writing endings to stories in a variety of genre.

LESSON TWO

WRITING

- Explain the lesson objective: *to write the end of 'Mountain Adventure' using paragraphs to organise action and feelings.*

- Recap the last paragraph of the story and how Butch was probably feeling at that time.

- Invite pupils to share their ideas about how the story might end.

- Talk a little about the effect these will have on Butch, and what feelings you will need to express.

- Choose two very different endings and note them on a flipchart or blank OHT. Note also how Butch is feeling at each stage.

- With pupils, organise the main themes of the ending into paragraphs, and make notes about how you will link them.

- Begin to write the first paragraph of one ending. Remind pupils about the use of complex sentences, and using sub-clauses to add detail. Model the use of commas in complex sentences.

Group activities: differentiation

All pupils plan how the story will end and write at least one paragraph of the story ending.

Lower attainers can continue the work from shared writing.

Guided writing. Help pupils build details and description into their sentences. Check that they understand how to link one paragraph to another.

Plenary

Ask some pupils to read their first paragraph and outline ending. Ask others to comment on the level of detail in the paragraph, and interesting words and phrases.

EXTENDED WRITING

1 Pupils finish the first draft of their story endings, then swap drafts with a partner and think about where they can add more detail.

2 Pupils present the work in its final form, including illustrations.

YOU WILL NEED

- Flipchart or blank OHT

ICT   For activities linked to this lesson see **PAGE 107**

WATCH OUT FOR

▸ Unclear structure to story.
▸ Weak links between paragraphs.
▸ Little description of setting and events.

79

MAIN WRITING OBJECTIVE

- **To identify the key features of impersonal writing (present tense and passive voice).**   6.3 T20

Word and sentence level objective

- To revise formal writing; impersonal voice; passive voice; complex sentences.   6.3 S3

LESSON ONE

MODEL TEXT

- Explain the lesson objective: *to identify the features of impersonal, formal language.*

- Read aloud Mr Robertson's letter. What clues tell you it is a formal letter? *form of address – Dear Sir/Madam; tone of letter – to the point; yours faithfully* Mark them on the OHT.

- Mark specific examples of formal language: e.g. *'constant refusal to provide appropriate parking', 'the Police have been informed'*

- Now look at Jeana Cunningham's letter. Ask pupils:
  - What differences can you see between these two letters? *language, purpose, audience*
  - What is the purpose of Jeana Cunningham's letter? *to thank someone*
  - Is it formal or informal? *less formal than Mr Robertson's, but not informal*

- Now read Claire's letter to her friend. Mark specific examples of informal language. *'Hope the deadly spots have gone', '(ha! ha!)'.*

Word and sentence level work

1 With pupils, highlight examples of passive verbs in Mr Robertson's letter: e.g. *'child hit by car', 'customers attracted by'.*
Change them into active form: e.g. *'car hits child', 'attracts customers'.* Discuss the effect.

2 Point out the complex sentences in the same letter. Look at connectives and linking phrases.

Group activities: differentiation

All pupils work in mixed ability groups using **PCM 52**.

Lower attainers complete question 1 only.

Guided reading. Work with **lower attainers** to discuss question 2 orally.

Plenary

Read aloud the second statement from **PCM 52**. Ask each group to say whether it is true or false, and to give reasons.

Take suggestions about how to make the informal sentences more formal.

YOU WILL NEED

- **OHT 27/OHT 28/OHT 29** – Formal and informal letters
- **PCM 52** – Formal and informal
- **PCM 53** – Homework

ICT For activities linked to this lesson see **PAGE 107**

HOMEWORK

Pupils use **PCM 53** to rewrite Claire's letter using formal language.

Link to reading objective

● To explore the features of impersonal, formal language.	6.3 T16

Assumed prior knowledge

● Awareness that language varies in different contexts.	6.2 T20
● Write individual or class letters for real purposes.	5.3 T17

Planning suggestion

You can make **formal writing** a theme for the week. Investigate a range of letters to look at their degree of formality. This unit can be linked to Unit 14.

LESSON TWO

WRITING

YOU WILL NEED
● Blank OHT or flipchart

- Invite two pupils to read their revised version of Claire's letter. Evaluate them against the criteria for formal writing.

- Explain the lesson objective: *to produce a piece of impersonal writing.*

- Tell pupils that together you will compose a formal letter. You can either choose an issue which pupils feel strongly about or focus on Claire's intention to write to the RSPCA. (You could link this exercise to Unit 14, Zoos.)

- Be sure that pupils understand the *purpose* and the *audience*.

- Revise how to set out a formal letter. Model writing the address, date, address of recipient and formal introduction.

- With pupils, decide on the purpose of each paragraph: *introduction of letter's purpose; description of conditions; what will happen next.*

- Plan the first paragraph together, introducing your reason for writing. Brainstorm some formal phrases before you begin: e.g. *I wish to draw your attention to...; I think that ... should be investigated*

- Model writing the first paragraph. Think aloud as you write. Ask pupils to suggest improvements: e.g. *active into passive verbs.*

Group activities: differentiation

In pairs, pupils plan and draft a second paragraph.

Higher attainers can go on to write the next paragraph.

Guided writing. Work with pupils at the drafting stage. Remind them of the need for formal language.

ICT For activities linked to this lesson see **PAGE 107**

Plenary

Invite some pupils to read aloud their work in progress. Others comment on the use of formal language.

EXTENDED WRITING

Pupils work independently to finish writing their letters.

They then produce a final, polished version of the letter and send it if appropriate.

WATCH OUT FOR
▶ Over-use of personal pronouns.
▶ Lapses from present tense.

23 Family Poems ● THEMATIC POEMS

MAIN WRITING OBJECTIVE

● **To write a sequence of poems linked by theme or form.**   6.3 T13

Word and sentence level objective

● To create similes and metaphors.   6.3 W7

LESSON ONE

MODEL TEXT

PB

● Explain the lesson objective: *to look at several poems linked by theme.*

● Ask pupils to scan the three poems in their books. What do they notice about them? *all written by the same person; all about people in her family*

● Read the three poems aloud. You could ask a fluent reader to read 'Dad'. Encourage them to really bring the words alive.

● Ask pupils:
– How are these poems similar? *all about poet's relatives; say a lot about the people; show how the poet feels about them*
– From whose point of view are all the poems written? *the poet as a child – e.g. 'I bring her my book'; fun and games with Dad*

OHT 30

● Look at 'My Sparrow Gran' in more detail. Ask pupils:
– What clues are there in the text to support the idea that Gran is like a sparrow? *e.g. 'singing', 'busy', 'brown-bright-eyed'.*
– How does Berlie Doherty convey the movement of a sparrow? *short sharp lines; short words – 'chats', 'darts', 'bits'; phrases such as 'scurries' (instead of rushes)*
– How is this poem a metaphor? *it portrays the gran as a sparrow*

Word and sentence level work

OHT 30

1 Look at the poem to find a simile *'arms that are feather-down warm'*

2 Ask pupils to suggest their own similes: e.g. *arms as warm as a piece of toast or a soft blanket.*

3 Change the simile into a metaphor: *Her arms are a soft, warm towel wrapped round me after a bath.*

Group activities: differentiation

PCM 54

All pupils complete both questions, using **PCM 54** for question 1.
Lower attainers could analyse one poem only.

Plenary

1 Invite groups to report back on their comparison of the poems. Each group reports about the feelings expressed in one poem.

2 Discuss the similarities of the three poems in mood or feeling: e.g. *the poet's sympathetic, kindly attitude to all of the characters.*

YOU WILL NEED

● **Pupil's Book** pages 72–73
● **OHT 30** – My Sparrow Gran
● **PCM 54** – Comparing the poems
● **PCM 55** – Homework

ICT For activities linked to this lesson see **PAGE 107**

HOMEWORK

Pupils make notes on **PCM 55** to describe the character of 'My Sparrow Gran'.

Link to reading objective

- To discuss how linked poems relate to one another by themes, format and repetition.

6.3 T2

Assumed prior knowledge

- To be able to analyse and compare poetic style, use of forms and themes of significant poets.

5.1 T7

- To write metaphors from original ideas or similes.

5.1 T17

- To analyse how feelings and moods are conveyed in poems.

6.2 T5

Planning suggestion

You can use this unit as the basis for a week of looking at and writing poems with a related theme. This unit can also be used to introduce the work of Berlie Doherty before going on to look at Unit 24.

LESSON TWO

WRITING

YOU WILL NEED

- Flipchart or blank OHT

- Ask pupils to feedback their homework notes. Make a list of words to describe Gran's personality, supported by quotes from the poem.

- Explain the lesson objective: *to write a short poem in the style of 'Grandpa'.*

- Choose a person who is well known to you and pupils: e.g. *caretaker.*

- Decide on two physical features of the person to describe in the opening lines of the poem: e.g. *eyes, smile, hair, hands.*

- Brainstorm words to describe the person's *eyes: e.g. blue, twinkling.*

- Choose a simile to complete the first line. Write the first line together.

- Add a second simile to make line 2.

- Compose the next two lines, by taking a second feature, e.g. *hands. Either* go through the same process to complete lines 3 and 4 using similes, *or* follow the original pattern and compose a metaphor.

Group activities: differentiation

All pupils write a short poem of their own based on 'Grandpa'.

Lower attainers write a poem with two similes (question 1). **Higher attainers** write a metaphor for lines 3 and 4.

Guided writing. Work with **lower attainers**, helping them draw up a list of descriptive words and developing each into a simile.

Plenary

Select pupils to read their own poems aloud. Other pupils listen and evaluate the description. Does the poem create a vivid picture of the person in your mind?

EXTENDED WRITING

Pupils should finish the poem begun in group activities, swap it with a partner and discuss possible improvements. They then present a final version for inclusion in an anthology.

ICT For activities linked to this lesson see **PAGE 107**

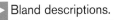

WATCH OUT FOR

▶ Bland descriptions.
▶ Unimaginative similes or metaphors.

Berlie Doherty – Talking to a Poet

● POETIC STYLE

MAIN WRITING OBJECTIVE

- **To write and compare poems, drawing out the different styles and preoccupations.**   6.3 T12

Word and sentence level objectives

- To revise language conventions and grammatical features of poetic texts.   6.3 S1
- To experiment with language, creating new similes and metaphors.   6.3 W7

LESSON ONE

MODEL TEXT

YOU WILL NEED
- **Pupil's Book** pages 75–76
- **PCM 56** – Two poems
- **PCM 57** – Homework (a)
- **PCM 58** – Homework (b)

- Explain the lesson objective: *to consider how a poet writes, by looking at her work.*

PB
- Read the interview with the poet Berlie Doherty. Ask pupils:

  – What do you think Berlie Doherty means when she says that a poem is like a flash of lightning? *comes suddenly, unexpectedly, a shock, very bright*

  – Can you think of some examples of abstract subjects? *love, war, loss, friendship*

  Relate these to Doherty's description of walking in Belfast. Explore how she uses real, 'concrete' experiences to inspire poetry about abstract things such as 'beauty' or 'peace'.

  – Why is poetry not just 'cut-up prose'? *more concentrated – every word is special, with its particular rhythms and music*

  – What does Berlie Doherty mean by 'a jewel in every line'? *something special, a rhythm that is just right, a word that says a lot in a little*

- Read aloud the poem 'The Wild White Horses'. Ask pupils to listen carefully for 'the rhythm and music of the words'.

Word and sentence level work

PB

1 'The Wild White Horses' is one long metaphor for the sea. Ask pupils to suggest similes for the sea.

2 Discuss what makes a poem 'formal': e.g. *patterns of rhythm, rhyme and line length, repeated phrases, formal language.*

Group activities differentiation

PCM 56

In pairs, pupils work to complete both questions using **PCM 56**.

Lower attainers could work on one poem only.

Guided reading. Discuss both poems with **lower attainers** and answer the questions orally.

Plenary

Ask pairs of pupils to read their favourite poem aloud and describe what it is about and how it makes them feel. Take a class vote on the favourite poem.

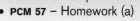

ICT   For activities linked to this lesson see **PAGE 107**

HOMEWORK

Ask pupils to look at 'Four Haiku' by Berlie Doherty. There are differentiated homework exercises on **PCM 57** (lower attainers) and **PCM 58** (higher attainers).

Link to reading objective

- To compare and contrast the work of a single writer.   6.3 T5

Assumed prior knowledge

- Author study Michael Morpurgo (Year 5, Units 10 and 11).
- Metaphors.
- Haiku.   4.3

Planning suggestion

You can make an author study of **Berlie Doherty** the theme for the week. You can start by using Unit 23, Family Poems. Try to look at examples of Berlie Doherty's prose and poetry. This unit also links to Unit 28.

LESSON TWO

WRITING

- Spend a few minutes sharing responses to the haiku read for homework.

- Berlie Doherty often works in schools. Re-read what she says about it in the last paragraph of the interview.

- Explain the lesson objective: *to write a poem, working in the way described by Berlie Doherty.*

- Start with a word (a noun). You could use 'star', or 'waterfall', or any other evocative word. Write it in the centre box on the OHT.

- Brainstorm words and phrases associated with your word. Write them around the centre box.

- Encourage pupils to suggest detail, using all their senses:

  – *How does it make you feel?*

  – *What does it remind you of?*

  – *Can you suggest any metaphors or similes to describe the word?*

- Explain to pupils that they will be using these notes to write their own poem. Remind them they do not need to look for rhymes. If they wish they could write a haiku.

Group activities: differentiation

All pupils work individually on the first draft of their poem using **PCM 59**. They then discuss it in their group.

Guided writing. Work with **lower attainers** to write a group poem.

Plenary

Ask a few pupils to read out their first drafts. Ask for positive comments – words or phrases which work well. Point out similarities and differences between the drafts. Explain that everyone's experience is unique.

EXTENDED WRITING

Pupils continue to work on the poems, revising and editing to produce a final version. Work on similes. Help pupils to build up to the emotion at the end. This could link to Unit 28, Berlie Doherty – Publishing

YOU WILL NEED

- **Pupil's Book** page 75
- **OHT 31** – Poem brainstorm
- **PCM 59** – Poem brainstorm

WATCH OUT FOR

- ▶ Imprecise, unevocative vocabulary.
- ▶ Superfluous words.
- ▶ Lack of focus.

PB

OHT 31

PCM 59

MAIN WRITING OBJECTIVE

- **To secure control of impersonal writing; sustained use of the present tense and the passive voice.** 6.3 T20

Word and sentence level objectives

- To revise formal styles of writing. 6.3 S3
- To search for, collect, and spell technical words derived from work in other subjects. 5.2 W9

LESSON ONE

MODEL TEXT

- Display the first OHT. Cover up everything except the title of the extract. Ask pupils what type of writing they think will follow.

- Reveal the whole text and read it aloud. Ask pupils which of the suggestions were correct, or nearly correct, and why.

- Explain the lesson objective: *to read an explanatory text and look at the features of style and vocabulary.*

- Look at the diagram on the second OHT. Ask a pupil to indicate a point on the diagram as you read the written explanation again.

- Look at **Prompt Chart 8 – Explanation**. Ask pupils which features David includes in his explanation. Mark them on the OHT.
  - What do we learn from the first statement? *what the explanation is about*

  - How has David organised his writing to explain what happens? *a series of numbered steps which explain the process in a logical order*

Word and sentence level work

1 Underline examples of words that refer to internal parts of the body: e.g. *trachea, lungs, bronchial tubes, alveoli, capillaries, heart.* Explain that they will be looking up the meaning of some of these words during group work.

2 Look for examples of pronouns (*it, they*) being used instead of a noun. Explain that these cut down repetition in a piece of writing. Ask pupils to say to what each pronoun refers.

3 Find examples of passive verbs. Ask pupils what effect these have. *make the writing impersonal*

Group activities: differentiation

In pairs, all pupils complete questions 1 and 2. They will need **PCM 60** for question 1. **Higher attainers** complete questions 3 and 4.

Plenary

Share the definitions of the technical words.

Ask pupils to find where a reason for something happening is given in the text. Remind pupils that a good explanation should not only say **what** happens but should also give reasons **why** it happens.

YOU WILL NEED

- **Pupil's Book** pages 78–79
- **OHT 32** – When we breathe: text
- **OHT 33** – When we breathe: diagram
- **Prompt Chart 8** – Explanation
- **PCM 60** – Definitions
- **PCM 61** – Homework: Red rain

 For activities linked to this lesson see **PAGE 107**

HOMEWORK

Pupils read the extract 'Red Rain in Mongolia' on **PCM 61** and draw and label a diagram to show what happened and why.

Link to reading objective

- To revise explanatory texts from year 5 term 2.   6.3 T15

Assumed prior knowledge

- Explanations.   5.2 T15
- Personal/impersonal language.   5.2 T21
- Formal/informal language.   6.2 S2

Planning suggestion

You can make **explanations – how and why things happen** a theme for the week. Research information linked to work in other subjects and write an explanation based on the research. Look at labelling and annotating diagrams.

LESSON TWO

WRITING

- Explain the lesson objective: *to plan and write a short explanation.*

- Remind pupils of the key features of an explanation, using **Prompt Chart 8**. Recap the features of a diagram: illustration, labels, arrows etc.

- Display the diagram of the water cycle. Ask pupils to describe the sequence of events. *water falls as rain or snow, runs down the rivers into the sea, evaporates into the air, forms clouds, falls as rain again*

- With pupils, plan and write an introductory statement to explain what the diagram is about.

- Decide what the first step of the explanation will be. Model the first step: i.e. *sea water heats up and rises as water vapour.*

- Write the next step. Encourage pupils to use connectives and complex sentences to make the explanation flow, and to give reasons for what happens: e.g. *Sea water heats up and rises as water vapour. Then the water vapour, as it rises, condenses into water droplets because it meets cooler air. The water droplets form clouds.*

Group activities: Differentiation

In pairs, pupils continue writing the explanation begun in shared writing. Leave the OHT on display.

Lower attainers can use the writing frame on **PCM 62** for support. **Higher attainers** could write their own version, beginning with their own opening statement.

They then swap work with a partner to check it.

Guided writing. Work with **higher attainers**, helping them to write complex sentences and to think about the reasons why things happen.

Plenary

Listen to some pupils reading their explanation of the water cycle. Ask other pupils to comment on which features of a written explanation have been included.

EXTENDED WRITING

Pupils revise and polish their explanations and make them into an information leaflet or poster.

YOU WILL NEED

- **Prompt Chart 8 –** Explanation
- **OHT 34 –** Water cycle diagram
- **PCM 62 –** Writing frame

ICT For activities linked to this lesson see **PAGE 107**

WATCH OUT FOR

- Lack of logical progression.
- Saying **what** happens but not **why**.

87

26

Book Blurbs • SYNOPSIS

MAIN WRITING OBJECTIVE

- **To write a brief synopsis of a text for a back cover blurb.**   6.3 T10

Word and sentence level objectives

- To practise and extend vocabulary.   6.3 W6
- To revise language conventions – persuasive texts.   6.3 S1

LESSON ONE

MODEL TEXT

- Explain the lesson objective: *to look at cover blurbs and see how they work on the reader.*

- Read aloud the back cover blurbs. Ask pupils:

  – What text type or genre are these books? *fiction; non-fiction (history)*

  – Which book would you most want to read and why?

  – What does a book blurb usually tell you? *fiction – brief outline of the plot; non-fiction – the subject outline, something about what you can find out from the book*

  – How do the blurbs try to persuade you to read or buy the book? *questions make you want to know the answer/cliffhangers*

  – Do you learn anything about the writers from the back covers? *The fiction writer is a prizewinner who has written other well-known books. The other writer is not mentioned at all.*

  – Can you think of the names of any non-fiction writers? Why do you think that non-fiction writers are not very well known? *They write in a less personal style, often written to order for the publisher*

Word and sentence level work

1 Look at the use of questions in the blurbs to stimulate interest.

2 Explore why leader dots are used. *they leave you in suspense*

3 Investigate the effect of capital letters, italics and different fonts.

Group activities: differentiation

All pupils use **PCM 63** to write a brief description of what they expect the two books to be about.

Lower attainers choose one book only.

Plenary

Ask pupils to predict the content, style and tone of the books from the blurbs.

YOU WILL NEED

- **Pupil's Book** pages 81–82
- **PCM 63** – What is it about?
- **PCM 64** – Homework

 For activities linked to this lesson see **PAGE 107**

HOMEWORK

Pupils look at three of their favourite books, fiction or non-fiction. Using **PCM 64**, they list all the details they find on the back cover.

Link to reading objective

- To describe and evaluate the style of an individual writer.   6.3 T1

Assumed prior knowledge

- Book reviews.   3.3 T14
- Flyers and advertisements.   4.3 T25
- Reading journal.   5.1 T13

Planning suggestion

You can use this unit as the basis for a week looking at book blurbs and publishers' catalogues. Pupils could write their own book blurbs and reviews for a library display.

LESSON TWO

WRITING

- Explain the lesson objective: *to write a back cover blurb for a book they have enjoyed.*

- Choose a popular class novel or a story that all the pupils know well. Remind pupils that the aim is to persuade other people that it is a book worth reading.

- Make notes about the main characters, events and themes.

- Begin to write the blurb together. Start with the main characters and story line. Point out that there is only space to write two or three sentences, and that it is quite difficult to sum up the information in a few words. Model how to prune and rearrange sentences. 'Think aloud' as you write.

- Ask pupils which part of the story would make a good cliffhanger.

- Try to find a suitable short quote from the text for the second box.

- Write one or two questions to tempt the reader to find out more, and add some information about the author.

- Pupils should now write their own book blurbs, using no more than 100 words.

Group activities: differentiation

All pupils plan the back cover blurb for a favourite book, fiction or non-fiction. They do not need to use the frames on **PCM 65** or **PCM 66** unless they choose to.

Guided writing. Help pupils to focus on key elements of the book and persuading others to read it.

Plenary

Ask some pupils to read out their plans. Remind them that they should make others want to read the book. How could they be improved?

EXTENDED WRITING

1 Pupils write their blurbs using their plans, then revise, polish and edit them.

2 Ask pupils to keep a record in their reading journal of 'best books'.

YOU WILL NEED

- Flipchart
- **OHT 35** – Writing Frame
- **PCM 65** – Writing Frame: fiction
- **PCM 66** – Writing Frame: non-fiction

ICT For activities linked to this lesson see **PAGE 107**

WATCH OUT FOR

▸ Giving too much of the plot away.
▸ Difficulty in summarising succinctly.

E-mail Etiquette • E-MAILS

MAIN WRITING OBJECTIVES

- **To select appropriate style and form to suit a specific purpose and audience.** 6.3 T22
- **To secure control of impersonal writing.** 6.3 T20

Word and sentence level objectives

- To practise and extend vocabulary. 6.3 W6
- To revise language conventions. 6.3 S1
- To investigate new language developments. 6.3 S2

LESSON ONE

MODEL TEXT

- Explain the lesson objective: *to think when you might choose to communicate by e-mail.*

- Sum up the main features of electronic mail:
  – Electronic mail allows you to send a written message via the telephone system.

  – To use e-mail you need an Internet address – you see them at the end of television programmes, on letterheads, on information leaflets: e.g. services@ginn.co.uk; sarah.jones@repp.co.uk.

- Read aloud 'E-mail Etiquette' and ask pupils:
  – How does e-mail differ from a letter or a telephone conversation? *you cannot see or hear people; you can answer much more quickly; you can send the message to several people at once; you can attach computer files; on the telephone you can respond to a person's mood and you know they have got your message*

- Look at the e-mail messages and ask pupils:
  – Who do you think wrote them?
  – Who do you think they were sent to?
  – Why do you think they were sent?

Word and sentence level work

1 Look at the personal shorthand in the e-mail messages. Why is it used? *it is more like speech ('byee')*

2 Ask pupils to contribute examples of computer jargon: e.g. *Internet, log on, online, desktop, website, mouse, floppy disk, download.* Discuss derivations – check in an up to date dictionary.

Group activities differentiation

In pairs, all pupils complete questions 1 and 2 using **PCM 67**. **Higher attainers** can move on to question 3.

Guided reading. Discuss the best way to send each message.

Plenary

Share ideas on which messages are not suitable to be sent by e-mail. Talk about why these other messages would be better sent by letter or discussed over the telephone.

YOU WILL NEED

- **Pupil's Book** pages 84–85
- **PCM 67** – E-mail messages
- **PCM 68** – Homework: Ways of sending messages

PB

PB

PB

PCM 67

ICT For activities linked to this lesson see **PAGE 108**

HOMEWORK

Pupils complete **PCM 68**, thinking about the suitability of different forms of communication.

Link to reading objective

- To review a range of text types, discussing when a writer might choose a given style and form.

6.3 T19

Assumed prior knowledge

- Some knowledge and awareness of e-mails.
- Letters, recounts and other forms of communication.

Planning suggestion

You can use this unit as part of a week looking at **different forms of communication**. Look at conventions of formal and informal letters (link to Unit 22) and e-mail messages. If possible, look at other forms of Internet communication.

LESSON TWO

YOU WILL NEED

- **OHT 36** – E-mail screen
- **PCM 69** – E-mail screen

WRITING

- Explain the lesson objective: *to compose an e-mail message.*
- If you have the facility, you can obviously do this for real.

- The OHT shows a computer screen with a blank e-mail message box. Look at some of the icons and talk about what they stand for (send, attach file etc.)
- Decide who you are sending the message to, and what subject you are going to write about. Pick something relevant to everyone: e.g. *contacting another school, contacting a publisher about a book, writing to a television programme.* Invent an e-mail address if you cannot find a real one, and write it on the OHT.
- Explain that the address is in two parts, separated by @, meaning 'at'. The first part is the **user's** name and the second part is the **domain** name – that is the name of the Internet server where the user has an account. Dots separate the different parts of the address.
- Explain that the e-mail system automatically tells the recipient who the message is from.
- Write the subject of your message on the subject line.
- With pupils, begin to draft a message. Think about how formal or informal it should be and any shorthand you could use.

Group activities differentiation

All pupils compose their own e-mail messages, using the blank format on **PCM 69**. **Lower attainers** could continue the subject from shared writing. They then swap with a partner and reply.

Guided writing. Help pupils to summarise the subject effectively for the subject line, and to edit the message for brevity.

 For activities linked to this lesson see **PAGE 108**

Plenary

Read out some of the e-mails. Are they written in an appropriate style?

EXTENDED WRITING

On the back of **PCM 68**, pupils list the advantages and disadvantages for each means of communication shown on the front. They can then write a balanced argument about one of the methods.

WATCH OUT FOR

▶ Lack of brevity.
▶ Poor grasp of overall subject for subject line.

MAIN WRITING OBJECTIVE

- **To write a sequence of poems linked by theme or form.** 6.3 T13

Word and sentence level objective

- To revise features of poetic texts. 6.3 S1

LESSON ONE

YOU WILL NEED
- **Pupil's Book** pages 87–88
- **PCM 70** – Homework

MODEL TEXT

- Recap or introduce the different people involved in the publishing process: publisher, commissioning editor, copy-editor, designer, illustrator, production team, printer.

- Explain that there are many things to think about when a writer publishes a poetry collection. A new edition of Berlie Doherty's book, *Walking on Air*, was recently published. New poems were added and it was re-illustrated.

- Read aloud the interview with the poet. Ask pupils:

  – What does the title *Walking on Air* make you think of? What does the phrase mean?

  – Does the order of the poems matter? Discuss how pupils read poetry collections – from beginning to end or jumping about?

- Briefly discuss the cover, blurb and the section from the contents list.

Word and sentence level work

1 Discuss the meaning of upper and lower case. Ask pupils why upper case would be used. *more emphasis, makes something look important*

2 *Walking on Air* is an everyday figure of speech. Collect other 'walking' and 'air' metaphors. Use a good dictionary. Examples include: *walking disaster/walking encyclopaedia/walk all over someone/walk away with/talking hot air/airy-fairy/up in the air/airhead.*

Group activities: differentiation

In pairs, all pupils complete question 1. **Higher attainers** can move on to question 2.

Guided reading. Do the second activity orally with **lower attainers**.

Plenary

Discuss the poems pupils would read first and why. Point out the use of typical features of advertising/persuasive language on the back cover blurb: e.g. *imperatives, description, present tense.*

ICT For activities linked to this lesson see **PAGE 108**

HOMEWORK

Pupils read the poem 'Playgrounds' on **PCM 70**. They think about how they would illustrate it in a published collection and then draw sketches.

Planning suggestion

You can use this unit as part of an author study week (links to Unit 23, Family Poems, and Unit 24, Berlie Doherty – Talking to a Poet). It can also be used as a starting point for writing poetry.

Link to reading objective

- To compare and contrast the work of a single writer. 6.3 T5

Assumed prior knowledge

- Interview with Berlie Doherty (Unit 24)
- Writing poetry.
- Back cover blurbs.

LESSON TWO

WRITING

YOU WILL NEED
- Poems written by pupils – as many as possible

- Explain the lesson objective: *to make group poetry collections.* (Pupils who are prolific writers might prefer to make their own individual collection and should be encouraged to do so.)

- Discuss the range of poetry that pupils have written during the year: e.g. *personification, conversation poems, nonsense poems, haiku, tanka, poem sequences.*

- Anticipate difficulties pupils may have in deciding which poems should be included in the group collections. Agree to abide by group majority votes, but everybody must have at least one poem included.

- Ask pupils to think about whether the poems can be linked by a theme.

- Explain that they will need to think of a suitable title for the collection. Encourage them to think of a title with several meanings like, *Walking on Air.*

- Pupils will need to design a front cover which uses the title and reflects the contents.

- Remind pupils that the back cover will need a blurb. Look at the examples in their books and recap the features of persuasive writing.

Group activities differentiation

All pupils work in groups to make and design an anthology of their poems, thinking of a suitable title.

If any groups do not have enough poems of their own for this activity, they can include poems from favourite poetry books.

Guided writing. Work with the group most likely to have problems in making decisions. Help them to think of a title with different meanings

ICT For activities linked to this lesson see **PAGE 108**

Plenary

Discuss progress so far and any difficulties encountered.

EXTENDED WRITING

Pupils continue to work on the poetry collections. Find time outside the lesson for illustrations and if possible, book-making. They should try to make the end product as professional as possible.

WATCH OUT FOR
▶ Rushed presentation.
▶ Lack of variety.

29

In the Stars! • HOROSCOPES

MAIN WRITING OBJECTIVE

- **To select the appropriate style and form to suit a specific purpose and audience.**　6.3 T22

Word and sentence level objectives

- To conduct language investigations through reading.　6.3 S2
- To extend vocabulary.　6.3 W6
- To invent words using known roots.　6.3 W5

LESSON ONE

MODEL TEXT

YOU WILL NEED
- **Pupil's Book** pages 90–91
- **OHT 37** – Horoscopes
- **PCM 71** – Horoscopes

- Explain the lesson objective: *to look at the features of magazine horoscopes and to read them critically.*

OHT 37
- Read aloud some of the horoscopes from the OHT. Ask pupils to identify the main features: *addressed to reader (second person), very generalised – could apply to lots of different circumstances.*

- Ask pupils why they think horoscopes are written in this way. *so that they can apply to anyone who reads them*

- Briefly discuss what areas of activity are predicted: *general themes such as luck, love, money, friendship.*

- Look at the symbols for each sign. What do pupils think they are? Explain their meanings, and that they are linked to constellations in the sky (hence 'stars').

Word and sentence level work

OHT 37
1 Identify the features which indicate the genre. Underline the vague terms: *'a certain someone', 'you want to try something ...' 'a friendship founders'*

2 Investigate 'horoscope'. Try to define it, then look up the dictionary definition. Find out the meaning of 'horo' and 'scope'. Collect other examples of '-scope' words: e.g. *telescope, microscope, kaleidoscope.*

3 Ask pupils to invent words using the same roots: e.g *horophobia.*

Group activities: differentiation

In pairs, all pupils complete questions 1 and 2.

PCM 71
Lower attainers can use **PCM 71** for support with question 2.

Higher attainers can move on to complete question 3.

Guided reading. Work with **lower attainers** to identify generalisations.

Plenary

Ask pupils to read out some of the generalisations they have found. Share whether pupils believe in the horoscopes and their reasons.

ICT For activities linked to this lesson see **PAGE 108**

HOMEWORK

Ask pupils to look for other examples of horoscopes in magazines and newspapers and bring them in.

Link to reading objective	
● To appraise a text quickly and efficiently.	6.3 T17

Assumed prior knowledge	
● Features of newspaper and magazine articles.	4.1 T20
● Letters for real purposes.	5.3 T17

Planning suggestion

You can use this unit as part of a week of looking at a variety of magazine articles.

LESSON TWO

WRITING

* Spend a few minutes looking at the examples of horoscopes that pupils have found at home. Pick out any points of interest: e.g. *useful phrases, layout, symbols.*

* Explain the lesson objective: *to design and write their own horoscope page.*

* Refer back to the horoscopes you looked at yesterday. Look briefly at the layout: e.g. *title, dates in brackets, zodiac signs.*

* Model the first stages of writing a horoscope page. Fill in the dates for each sign.

* With pupils, start composing the text for one sign, modelling the use of vague generalisations, chatty style, idioms, dire hints and good news: e.g. *Moodwise, you'll find yourself blowing hot and cold this week. The only way to get back on an even keel is to chat with a pal.*

* Explain that they will work in groups to produce their own horoscope page, with each pupil writing two horoscopes. Encourage group responsibility – agreeing democratically, contributing to careful presentation and assembly of the separate pieces of text into a complete page. Tell them to keep the content light-hearted.

Group activities: differentiation

In groups of six, each pupil drafts two horoscopes and designs the symbols for both. Pupils decide who will write which horoscopes and who will design the title and headings for the enlarged A3 page, **PCM 72**

Guided writing. Help pupils to think of suitable generalisations and to use a chatty style.

Plenary

Ask groups to read out one of their draft horoscopes. Encourage positive comment.

EXTENDED WRITING

Pupils can finish and revise the horoscopes, and make a final illustrated copy of each to paste onto the A3 sheet.

YOU WILL NEED
* **OHT 38** – Blank horoscope
* **PCM 72** – Blank horoscope (enlarged to A3)

 For activities linked to this lesson see **PAGE 108**

WATCH OUT FOR
▶ Failure to use general terms.
▶ Inappropriate tone.

30

Writing to Time ● SHORT STORY

MAIN WRITING OBJECTIVE

● **To write an extended story.** 6.3 T14

Word and sentence level objectives

● To revise narrative language conventions. 6.3 S1
● To secure control of complex sentences. 6.3 S4
● To practise and extend vocabulary. 6.3 W6

LESSON ONE

MODEL TEXT

● Explain the lesson objective: *to think about ways to help yourself write a story to time.*

● Explain that writing to time is an important skill. It is especially difficult to plan and write a short story in just 45 minutes, but it is important to practise for the writing tests at the end of the year. This unit offers some tips.

● Read aloud the tips about writing to time. Ask pupils:

– Why do you think it is sensible to limit the number of characters?

– What happens if you forget to tell the reader something they need to know? *The reader cannot follow the story.*

– Why do you think the beginning should be short? *to get into the action straight away*

– How could you 'feed something about the end into the beginning'?

● Discuss which parts of a story pupils find most difficult to write.

Word and sentence level work

1 Discuss the usefulness of looking at possible ways of spelling a word by writing them down.

2 Recap rules for new paragraphs – to show a change of some kind: change of place; change in time; change of speaker; change of subject.

3 Quickly brainstorm a variety of connectives as alternatives for 'then'; or alternative verbs for 'said'.

Group activities differentiation

In pairs, pupils evaluate a pupil's writing for a SATs test (see **PCM 73**).

All pupils complete questions 1 to 3. **Higher attainers** can move on to question 4.

Guided reading. Help pupils to focus on the lack of resolution or character development in the story.

Plenary

How well does the story follow the tips? Can pupils suggest any improvements?

YOU WILL NEED

● **Pupil's Book** pages 93–94
● **PCM 73** – The Purple Pen Story
● **PCM 74** – Homework: Character profiles

ICT For activities linked to this lesson see **PAGE 108**

HOMEWORK

Using **PCM 74**, pupils make notes about two characters – one male, one female. They base them on people they know of about their age.

● To look at connections and contrasts in the work of different writers.   6.3 T6

Assumed prior knowledge

Considerable experience in writing narrative e.g.
● Stories with an issue.   4.3
● Alternative endings.   4.3
● Story openings.   5.1
● Narration.   6.1
● Story within a story.   6.2

Planning suggestion

You can use this unit to help pupils practise structuring an extended story and writing to time.

LESSON TWO

WRITING

● Explain to the pupils that the timing of the lesson will be different because they are going to write on their own without interruption for 45 minutes.

● Read the test instructions and make sure pupils are clear about what to do before they start work.

● Explain that they can use the character profiles they wrote for homework if they wish.

Group activities: differentiation

PCM 75

All pupils work individually on the same task, writing a story similar to those set in SATs tests. They can use **PCM 75** to plan the story.

Guided writing. Offer unobtrusive encouragement to the lowest attaining pupils.

Plenary

Discuss briefly what pupils liked and disliked about the experience. What did they learn from it? Did the tips help?

EXTENDED WRITING

Spend a subsequent writing session working on a pupil's story, evaluating it and revising where necessary. Pupils then revise their own work.

YOU WILL NEED

● **PCM 75** – Planning sheet

WATCH OUT FOR
▶ Limited development of character.
▶ Lack of variety in use of connectives.
▶ Lack of clarity.

Information and Communication Technology

ICT and its place in the UK Curriculum

The curricula for England, Wales, Scotland and Northern Ireland all require that ICT should be used to support writing and learning about language. The Literacy Hour is an ideal starting place for many of these activities. By incorporating ICT activities into the Literacy Hour and other writing sessions, many elements of the ICT Programmes of Study may be taught in 'real' contexts.

The new National Curriculum Orders for England & Wales (published in 1999 for implementation in 2000), the new 5 – 14 Guidelines for Scotland (published in 2000) and the Education Technology Strategy 1996-2000 in Northern Ireland, all give ICT a prominent place across all curriculum areas and give an entitlement for all pupils to achieve ICT capability.

ICT and Literacy

Literacy in the 21st century involves making sense of language and writing in many different contexts. In responding to texts, children must learn to recognise and be critical of the rich range of media; in producing their own writing, they must learn to use different media appropriately to suit their audience and purpose.

Children should be encouraged to explore the extent to which page-layout and design, use of colour, choice of fonts and text styles can enhance their writing. They also have opportunities, through the world wide web and multimedia authoring, to publish for wider audiences and to communicate via e-mail with children throughout the world.

During the Literacy Hour, pupils may be using ICT to support language and literacy development as well as developing their personal ICT capability.

Opportunities to develop the ICT skills associated with these activities can be included in the Literacy Hour and at other times throughout the week. The suggested activities provided in **Models for Writing** offer some starting points.

ICT to support whole class and group work

ICT can support and enhance discursive and interactive whole-class teaching and group work. The range of software available varies from fairly straightforward presentation packages available with standard office-type applications to fully-featured multimedia authoring tools. Interactive whiteboards, wide-format monitors, an LCD tablet with high-powered OHP, daylight projectors or large TV monitors should all be considered as options for presenting to groups. These vary considerably in price and are likely to represent significant capital investments for many primary schools. Teachers should discuss the options available with the ICT Co-ordinator or local advisory service.

When planning to use presentation software, consider what the 'added value' will be to pupils over traditional methods such as big books, flip-charts, blackboard and chalk, video, TV, radio, OHT, whiteboard and marker pen. A major advantage is that your presentation is stored in digital form and may be re-used for other purposes. If your presentation includes input from children during the session, this will also be stored for future use. Furthermore, a multimedia presentation allows a range of media to be used from one single workstation rather than juggling between an OHP, video and big book.

Models for Writing is accompanied by a set of colour OHTs which are an integral part of shared reading and writing. The OHTs contain extracts from model texts, and provide a wide variety of writing and planning frames to support pupils in developing their reading and writing skills. They allow the teacher to model both the reading and the writing processes to the class, and OHT pens can be used to highlight teaching points.

Audio-recording equipment is another valuable ICT tool. For example, when discussing performance poetry it may be used to enable children to experiment with different styles of delivery, evaluating each others' recordings.

ICT for writing, editing and publishing

Using ICT to support children's writing means far more than simply asking them to word-process their text. The use of ICT can help children compose, transform and present text, and will give them a growing understanding and confidence in literacy, language, layout, style and design. Whether the writing and presentation of a text involves illustrating a poem, setting out information in a chart, or annotating a diagram, ICT can be used to support the activity and examples are provided in *Models for Writing*.

When writing, the children can change their work using various tools. Cutting and pasting paragraphs, sentences and words gives children the freedom to experiment with their text and decide the most appropriate way of ordering it. Using the electronic thesaurus allows the children to expand their vocabulary, and the spell-checker gives them the opportunity to check and correct their work. The final piece of writing will have a high standard of presentation that has been developed and adapted to suit the audience and the purpose of the piece.

As far as you are able, it is important to choose appropriate software for these activities. Some word-processing packages are capable of handling text and images to produce more sophisticated work, but if you want the children to begin to learn transferable skills associated with desktop publishing (DTP) you will achieve far better results with a desktop publishing program than with a word-processor.

Teachers who are confident with computers, and who have the appropriate painting or drawing software can also consider the use of ICT to illustrate children's work, where such an activity supports the learning objective.

Writing and the Internet

The Internet provides many opportunities for developing communication skills. Children should think about the emerging styles of writing which are appropriate for e-mail messages and be given opportunities to send and receive e-mail for real purposes. They may have 'net-pals' who will be interested in some of the writing arising from the activities in *Models for Writing*. Some of the activities lend themselves to setting up an e-mail project between schools in the UK using this scheme, or using a unit in the scheme as the starting point for a project with schools in other parts of the world.

Preparing some writing for the school website is another means whereby children will be writing for real and wider unknown audiences. There are two ways in which pupils may 'publish' on the web. They may have produced some writing for print which may be 'showcased' in a gallery on the school website. There may also be opportunities for children to design part of the school website or even their own website.

ICT and *Models for Writing*

On pages 102–108 you will find ICT activities for each unit of *Models for Writing*.

On pages 109–112 you will find a **Glossary of ICT terms**. This explains the ICT terminology used in the activities and gives simple, practical examples of what the terminology means.

Preparation and organisation of activities

In preparing to use ICT with *Models for Writing* teachers should check with the ICT Co-ordinator what hardware and software are available for use with Year 6. It is important to plan the development of ICT resources in consultation with other teachers, the Literacy Co-ordinator and ICT Co-ordinator. Many of the activities and resources prepared for use in one year group may be quickly modified for use by colleagues in other year groups if there is a school-wide policy on how to create and store digital material.

The ICT Co-ordinator will be able to advise on the most appropriate software to use for different applications, in particular when graphics are being created and stored.

Another important co-ordination function is to ensure that children have had the opportunity to learn the basic ICT skills they will need to use in order to carry out some of the activities suggested in *Models for Writing*.

The time taken to prepare the ICT activities for *Models for Writing* will depend on the ICT competence and confidence of teachers, as well as the software and hardware available in school. It may be appropriate for non-teaching assistants to do some of the preparatory tasks under the direction of a Year 6 teacher. Once the basic preparation is done, the resources will be available to, and may be modified and adapted for each class.

It is important to plan how to develop, save and back-up all ICT resources using a systematic and agreed filing structure either on floppy disks or a school network. Discuss the systems with the ICT Co-ordinator and develop a whole-school approach to managing digital resources.

IMPORTANT NOTE:

Several of the following ICT activities instruct you to prepare a text-file of the model text.

It is important to be aware that the keying in and electronic storage of copyright material is a breach of copyright law. The Publisher has obtained permission for the classroom activitites suggested in *Models for Writing*, but the keyed texts should not be stored on a network or otherwise transferred electronically.

If in doubt, consult your Copyright and Licensing Authority document.

Models for Writing: ICT activities

(Please note that these do not include the use of OHTs, which are within the main lesson plans for each unit.)

UNIT	TITLE	LESSON ONE	LESSON TWO
1	Big Bad Wolf	Prepare a **text file** of a traditional story, for example *Hansel and Gretel* or *Cinderella*, bringing out the character of a 'villain'.	Open two **word-processing** documents and split the window to view both a new, blank document and the prepared text file. Pupils re-write the story from the villain's viewpoint in the blank document by cutting and pasting copy from the original, making changes as appropriate and saving the new file regularly.
2	Double Act	Prepare a **text file** of the model text. Using the text file, pupils revise it to form a narrative from the point of view of Ruby or Garnet.	Prepare a three-column **table** in a word-processor in which to summarise the points of view of the two narrators. One column headed 'main events' the other two headed with the name of each narrator. Using the first person, pupils write a short statement in each narrator's column for each event.
3	Eclipse of the Sun	Use an **Internet search engine** or suitable CD-ROM to find out detailed information on subjects chosen for the homework task. **Download** and save text and references. Save good sites as **bookmarks** or **favourites**. Discuss issues of authenticity, accuracy and copyright when using web-based resources.	Using 'outline' view in a **word-processor** provides useful support for drafting ideas for a report. Save the paragraph headings suggested by pupils into a text file to use as starting points for writing and research. Working in pairs or threes, pupils draft their reports in 'outline'.
4	Food, Glorious Food	Pupils audio-record short interviews with lunchtime supervisors and kitchen staff talking about 'my memorable meal'. (Brief the staff first, giving them some background about the lesson objectives.)	Pupils transcribe the recordings, using a **word-processor** and write in autobiographical style on behalf of the interviewee. The interviewees should be asked to check the printed drafts. Pupils revise the interviews and check the autobiographical style is maintained.

UNIT	TITLE	LESSON ONE	LESSON TWO
5	I Met at Eve	Create a two column **table** in a word-processor to list poetic language and definitions. Children start the list using examples from this Unit. Sort the list alphabetically in the word-processor and print the first drafts for discussion.	Build the list up as a class activity during work on poetry, saving it regularly and revising definitions.
6	Beowulf	Prepare a **text file** of the model text. Pupils prepare storyboards of the scenes from the model text in preparation for making a radio adaptation of the story.	Pupils collect or make suitable sound samples using a computer and microphone, saving them in appropriate formats. Record the story, incorporating the sound effects directly into a computer.
7	In the News	Using a **word-processor** or text-editor, pupils draft and revise reports about Beowulf. (The model text prepared for Unit 6 may be useful to support pupils' writing.)	Prepare a template in a **DTP** package with **image boxes** and **text frames** suitable for a newspaper front page. Children import the copy, lay up the pages and use suitable images to illustrate the page.
8	Summing Up	Prepare a **text file** of the model text (the english, maths and science comments). Using the prepared text and a **word-processor** pupils summarise Jane's report in 50 words. Check word-length with the **word count** facility. If the word-processor has a summarise facility, test this out on Jane's report.	Prepare a **word-bank** of subject vocabulary and statement banks of typical 'school report' phrases. Using the word-bank and statement banks, pupils draft a school report using a **word-processor**. Discuss the issues raised by using these automated 'statement banks'. How does the finished report differ from those hand-written by teachers? How do pupils feel about 'automated' reporting systems?

UNIT	TITLE	LESSON ONE	LESSON TWO
9	Harriet Tubman	Prepare a **text file** of the model text. Using the prepared text and a **talking word-processor**, pupils re-write Harriet's story as an autobiography.	Go to an **Internet search engine** and enter the keywords <Florence AND Nightingale>. Browse the sites, download and save relevant information, remembering to keep references and bookmark the sites. Discuss issues of authenticity and accuracy when using web-based resources. Using a word-processor and the saved information from their search, pupils write a short biography of Florence Nightingale's life.
10	Samuel Pepys	Prepare a **word-bank** of vocabulary associated with a recently studied history topic.	Using the **word-bank** and a **talking word-processor**, pupils draft a short diary entry for the historical event. Save the drafts. Use the collection of drafts to prepare a detailed autobiographical account of the event, using appropriate language from the period, including spellings if appropriate and retaining chronological accuracy.
11	Alexander's Story	A branching story is one where you can make choices about how the story/play progresses, and/or ends. **Hyperlinking** is an ideal way to develop these types of story. Pupils browse some 'branching stories' on CD-ROM, thinking about the links and the 'story within a story' – this may be a small group or whole class activity.	Pupils create a storyboard to show how Alexander's Story could be re-created as a branching story. Write new events for some of the key points where there are choices: the evacuation, calling out when the gate is shut, the stray bomb, meeting Alexander, going to the Head. Using a **multimedia authoring package**, create the branching story.
12	Beach Party	Prepare a **text file** of the model text (extract two).	Pupils scan the text and highlight phrases which are typical features of popular horror. Pupils either revise the story of Vince and Jerry, adding dialogue and changing the characteristics of the surfers; or they can write a story of similar length involving two new characters.

UNIT	TITLE	LESSON ONE	LESSON TWO
13	What do you read and why?	Agree with the class what questions the survey is intended to answer. Using a **data-handling package**, pupils work on questionnaire designs based on the discussion of the model text, using checkboxes, option menus, yes/no, free text boxes etc. Print off and pilot the questionnaires with another class and revise in the light of feedback.	Print the final version of the questionnaires and circulate to other classes for completion. Enter data into the data handling package and interrogate the results. Discuss the extent to which the questionnaire served its intended purpose and how ICT supported the task (presentation of questionnaire, automated analysis, range of interrogation options, automated generation of charts).
14	Zoos	Prepare a **text file** of the model text. Using a **word-processor**, pupils re-write the model text either as an argument for or against keeping animals in captivity.	
15	Island of Horror	**Hyperlinking** enables authors and publishers of adventure games to create exciting environments to explore on CD-ROM and the Internet. Discuss some of the CD-based adventure games pupils have played. What makes them exciting? In what ways are CD-based games different from books of this genre?	Pupils create a storyboard for the *House of Horrors* in preparation for creating a multimedia game. Decide who will design and write the pages. Use **painting and drawing packages** to create illustrations, navigation buttons and icons. Use a **word-processor** or text-editor to write the elements of the storylines. Print them out for testing hyperlinks on the storyboard. Using a **multimedia authoring package**, build the adventure game.
16	All for an Ice Cream	Prepare a **word-bank** and statement bank of vocabulary and phrases associated with the weather to support poetry-writing.	Using a **talking word-processor**, write metaphorical poems about the weather.

UNIT	TITLE	LESSON ONE	LESSON TWO
17	Keep off the grass!	Demonstrate the use of fonts, styles, effects, white space and colour in an object-based drawing package. Discuss how these effects may be used to show instructions, information, rules and persuasion in notices. Discuss the comparative costs of printing in colour or black-only, from a printer or photocopier.	Pupils use an object-based **drawing package** to design notices for different parts of the school. Print out draft notices using different fonts and styles and discuss design issues with the group or class. Pupils print final notices in black or colour, depending on their purpose and siting. Discuss the durability of notices: do they need to last a few days or longer?
18	Singing my Song	Prepare **text files** of some haiku and tanka marked up to show syllables. A talking word-processor will provide support for pupils in writing their own tanka.	
19	Bun Stew	Prepare a **text file** of the model text 'Spellbound'. Pupils run this through a **spell checker** and change the spellings. Print it out and compare with the original.	Pupils try writing their own 'Spell Chequer' poem. Use a **word-processor** and **spell checker**. Print it out and ask other pupils to comment. Discuss some of the issues about the use of spell checkers raised by this activity. How much do you need to know about spelling to make effective use of a spell-checker.
20	The Earth Centre	Browse some **websites** to find information about local attractions. The British Tourist Authority may be a good place to start http://www.visitbritain.com it has lots of interesting links and an interesting design. Get paper-based literature about these places if possible. Compare the presentation of attractions on paper and the web. Discuss the differences in terms of design: bring out some of the technical differences in design for print or the web.	Using **web-authoring software**, pupils design a Home Page for the guide agreed upon in Shared Writing. Pupils identify the navigation buttons which will be needed to link with other parts of the website. Sketch a site plan showing links, navigation and headings for pages on other levels in the website.

UNIT	TITLE	LESSON ONE	LESSON TWO
21	Mountain Adventure	Prepare a **text file** of the model text.	Using a **talking word-processor** will provide support for writing. Pupils scan the text and highlight connecting words. They then re-write sections of the model text using simple sentences.
22	Dear Sir/Madam	Browse the **Internet**, using a **search engine**, to find contact details for organisations who represent issues of interest to the class. http://www.wspa.org.uk/home.html (World Society for the Protection of Animals) and http://www.rspca.org.uk (RSPCA) may be good places to start. Store the list of sites as **favourites** or **bookmarks** for other pupils to refer to.	Pupils select a suitable letter **template** in a **word-processor** to draft a formal letter to the RSPCA or other organisations representing an issue of interest to the class. Discuss why they selected the template. In particular discuss suitable fonts and layout for formal letters.
23	Family Poems	Prepare a **template** in a **DTP** package with **image boxes** and **text frames** to create a class anthology of the verses and illustrations produced in this Unit.	Browse the **Internet** for sites with poetry anthologies and recommend a suitable selection to the children. http://www.bbc.co.uk/education/listenandwrite/home.htm
24	Berlie Doherty – Talking to a Poet	Go to http://www.nawe.co.uk and invite a poet to come into school or discuss their ideas by e-mail.	
25	How we Breathe	Pupils discuss how best to present the water cycle as a **multimedia presentation**, putting their ideas onto a storyboard. Pupils prepare diagrams and buttons or icons in a drawing package and text in a word-processor to illustrate the water cycle.	Using **multimedia authoring software**, pupils produce an explanation of the water cycle with buttons or icons to link the diagram and text. It may be appropriate to include sound samples or voice-overs. Discuss how this is an effective way to present the information.
26	Book Blurbs	Using a **word-processor** or text editor with word count facility, pupils draft and refine a book blurb making sure that it does not exceed 100 words.	Prepare a **template** in a **DTP** package with **image boxes** and **text frames** suitable for a book cover blurb page. Children import their copy and use suitable images to illustrate the blurb.

UNIT	TITLE	LESSON ONE	LESSON TWO
27	E-mail Etiquette	E-mail links with another school would provide children with first-hand examples of using e-mail for real communication. There are many sites which offer 'partner-finding' services.	Try the partner-finding area of the Europen Schoolnet website at http://www.en.eun.org/menu/projects/partners.html or set up a local project in the LEA with other schools using *Models for Writing*.
28	Berlie Doherty – Publishing Poetry	Prepare a **template** for the anthology in a **DTP** package with **image boxes** and **text frames**. Use an optical character reader (OCR) to scan the selected poems into a word-processor or text editor. Pupils use the template to create their group anthology.	Pupils prepare illustrations in a **drawing** or **painting package**, or scan images they have already drawn, scanning text into a text-editor or word-processor from hand-written poems. This should be a group activity with pupils taking specialist roles such as designer, editor, illustrator, proof-reader etc.
29	In the Stars!	Prepare a **template** for the horoscopes page in a **DTP** package with **image boxes**, **text frames** and a suitable selection of **fonts**. Work together to create a statement bank and word bank in the style of horoscope writing.	Pupils use the **template** to lay up their horoscopes page. They prepare images for the signs of the zodiac in a drawing or painting package, basing them on the traditional signs. This should be a group activity with pupils taking specialist roles such as designer, editor, author, researcher, illustrator, proof-reader etc.
30	Writing to Time	Go to http://www.nawe.co.uk and invite an author to come into school to talk about writing to deadlines and building up ideas quickly.	

Glossary of ICT terms

All teachers will need to understand and use the vocabulary associated with ICT and help children to use it appropriately and in context.

This list provides a broad summary of terms and acronyms which will be needed to provide support for children at Key Stage 2.

Address: the unique identifier for a web page. Typically an address takes the form http://www.repp.co.uk and should be entered into the address bar on the browser window. In this example, <repp.> is the name of the company owning the website, <co.> indicates that it is a company (others include <org.> for organisation, <gov.> for government, <sch.> for school, <ac.>for university etc.) and <uk> indicates the country. No country code usually indicates a US based website or a site, which regards itself as international.

Application: a piece of software, usually installed onto the computer or run over a network.

Attachment (see enclosure): a file sent with an e-mail message. An attachment may be text, graphics or sound. It may be helpful to imagine them as 'paper-clipped' to a file as a note may be attached to a paper document.

Authoring software (see presentation software): an application which enables the user to create documents using mixed media including text, still and moving images, and sound, with a means of moving between pages or screens. These packages may be used to produce presentations for use in the classroom or hall, as well as for creating web pages.

Back up: to make copies of documents or applications on another disk or tape as a safeguard against data loss. It is essential to keep regular back ups. Check the school policy with the ICT Co-ordinator.

Bookmark (see favourite): to store the address of a web page in a list in order to return to it during another session browsing the world wide web.

Browse: to move from page to page on a website or CD-ROM.

Browser software: an application which displays the pages of a website. The two major browser applications are Microsoft *Internet Explorer* and *Netscape Navigator*.

Clip art: images available commercially or as free collections distributed on disks, CD-ROM or the Internet, which may be incorporated into documents, multimedia presentations and websites.

Cut and paste: to move text or images from a document and place them in another part of the same document or into another document.

Database software: an application which enables the user to set up fields and records containing data, and to sort the data and display the information in a number of ways including graphs and charts.

Daylight projector: a piece of equipment which projects the display from a computer onto an external screen. The projectors may be wall- or ceiling-mounted or stand-alone portable devices.

DTP (desktop publishing) software: an application which enables the user to combine text and graphics, using templates for page-layout and styles. Text and graphics are typically placed in text or picture frames after having been originally created in word-processing, text-editing, painting or drawing packages.

Digital: information which is held in numerical form. Typically, in a computer, this is as a sequence of binary numbers.

Directory: a folder on the desktop which contains documents and sub-directories enabling users to organise their work, and find documents and applications easily. The directory system is often likened to a filing cabinet, with drawers, sub-divisions and folders.

Document: a single piece of work. A document may be in a word-processor, desktop publisher or database application. Each document must be saved with a unique filename.

Download: to save material such as text, images or software from another computer, the Internet or a network, and store it locally for future use on a hard disk or school network.

E-mail (electronic mail): a service provided on the Internet whereby electronic messages may be sent by one user to one or many other users throughout the world in a few minutes at minimal cost. In order to use e-mail, users will need to have e-mail software and a profile set up which includes a personal e-mail address.

Enclosure (see attachment): a file sent with an e-mail message. An enclosure may be text, graphics or sound.

Favourite (sometimes spelled favorite, see bookmark): to store the address of a web page in a list in order to return to it during another session browsing the world wide web.

Filename: the name used when saving a document as a file. It is important to use filenames that you and others will understand when sharing documents on a network or creating collections of digital resources.

Font: a set of type characters in the same style. A font will include different weights (bold, light, book) and different slants (italic, oblique). There are numerous fonts, some will be supplied with each application, others may be purchased or obtained from free collections.

Graphic: an image or picture.

Hyperlink: the electronic link to related information (text, graphics, sound, entire documents, whole pages or websites) which enables users to browse the Internet or a CD-ROM by making their own choices about routes through the material. The cursor will usually change from an arrow to, for example, a hand icon when it is over a hyperlink. Hyperlinks are often highlighted in some way such as underlining. Clicking on a hyperlink takes the user to the related page or website.

Image box (or image frame): the placeholder for a graphic, picture or image in a document.

Interactive whiteboard: a large, touch-sensitive board onto which an image of the computer desktop is projected. Users can interact with the projected image by drawing on the board with a stylus.

ISP (Internet service provider): the company providing Internet services such as e-mail and access to the world wide web for a school, organisation, business or household. Some ISPs do not charge for their services but may carry advertising. Check with your ICT Co-ordinator how to access Internet services from school.

Internet: the network of networks. Networks are formed by connecting computers. The Internet has been formed by connecting networks into a global network of networks. It provides a set of protocols which allow different networks to talk to each other, and services such as e-mail and the world wide web.

Intranet: a closed, private network or network of networks which uses the same protocols as the Internet and provides the same services such as e-mail.

LCD (liquid crystal display) panel: a flat screen display which can be used with a high powered overhead projector for presentations to groups.

Multimedia: the presentation of information through the use of more than one medium e.g. text, sound, images.

Network: formed by connecting computers in order to share files and applications. Networks are either peer-to-peer where any computer can talk to any other computer on the network or client/server where one computer holds all the files and applications and can be accessed by the client computers.

Optical character recognition (OCR) software: an application which enables a scanner to 'read' text and convert it into a digital form. Once saved, the text may be exported to a word-processor for editing.

PDF (portable document format): a proprietary document file format, for which a reader is freely available from Adobe, which has been designed to ensure that documents, particularly DTP documents retain all their formatting and typographic styles and effects when viewed on another computer.

Presentation software (see authoring software): an application which enables the user to create documents using mixed media including text, still and moving images and sound with a means of moving between pages or screens. These packages may be used to produce presentations for use in the classroom or hall.

Scanner: a piece of equipment which enables users to copy paper-based materials such as photographs or illustrations and save them in digital format. A scanner produces a bitmap image composed of pixels and works in a similar way to a photocopier. Many scanners include OCR software as standard.

Search engine: a service provided commercially on the Internet used to search for documents on the Internet. Users access the search engine from a web page on the providers website by entering key words. The service is usually free to the user and paid for by advertising.

Spell-checker: a function available in most word-processors and many other software applications which enables users to check spelling. It is important to remember that spell-checkers use a dictionary stored on the computer and will search it for logical matches. Users will need a certain basic level of spelling strategies to be able to make use of this facility. A spell-checker will not pick up mis-spelt words that are in the wrong context (for example, 'there' and 'their'). Some software has grammar checkers which teachers should consider using with care. Check what conventions are used. The problem with many grammar and spell-checker software is that is uses US English, although there may be opportunities to customise the dictionaries.

Stylesheet (see also template): 'blank' documents which may be saved to include margins, text styles, headers, footers, page-numbering, guidelines, image frames and text boxes amongst many other features which may be set up so that every page has a common format.

Table: a function available in some word-processors and spreadsheets to organise lists into tables. These may then be sorted according to various criteria such as date, alphabetical order, number etc. Tables should be used in preference to the <tab> key when putting lists into a word-processor.

Talking word-processor: speech output is available in some word-processing packages. The user may hear individual letters, words or complete sentences as they are keyed in, or on demand. This is very valuable as support for reading and writing activities.

Template: 'blank' documents which may be saved to include margins, text styles, headers, footers, page-numbering, guidelines, image frames and text boxes amongst many other features which may be set up so that every page has a common format. They are essential for use in desktop publishing packages and useful for word-processing. When writing more than a short paragraph, it is 'good practice' to set up styles for the entire document rather than make 'local' changes to, for example, centre and embolden a heading.

Text file: any file which contains plain text. When transferring text between different applications and computer platforms, it is advisable to select rich text format (RTF) from the save options.

Text frame (text box): the placeholder for text in a desktop publishing document.

Thesaurus: a function available in many word-processing applications for finding a synonym, an antonym, or related words for a selected word in the user's text.

Typing tutor: an application which trains users to touch type, typically using a structured 'drill' approach with on-screen copy to practise typing from.

Undo: a useful feature available in most software applications. Reverses the last action and may be used more than once in some applications to retrace a series of actions.

Website: a collection of pages published on the world wide web.

Word count: a function available in many word-processing applications for automatically counting the number of words, pages, characters and lines in a selected part of the document or the entire document.

Word-bank: a collection of words, customised by the user and stored in a word-processor. Many word-processors designed for the education market have word-bank facilities whereby selected groups of words and phrases may be saved and used to support writing. Check with the documentation in the program available for how to create and save word-banks.

Word-processing software: an application which enables users to manipulate text.

World wide web: an Internet service which provides information in the form of pages which can include text, images, video clips and sound. These are viewed using a web browser.